New Directions for
Community Colleges

Arthur M. Cohen
EDITOR-IN-CHIEF

Richard L. Wagoner
ASSOCIATE EDITOR

Edward Francis Ryan
Gabriel Jones
MANAGING EDITORS

Student Tracking in the Community College

Trudy H. Bers
EDITOR

Number 143 • Fall 2008
Jossey-Bass
San Francisco

STUDENT TRACKING IN THE COMMUNITY COLLEGE
Trudy H. Bers (ed.)
New Directions for Community Colleges, no. 143

Arthur M. Cohen, Editor-in-Chief
Richard L. Wagoner, Associate Editor

NEW DIRECTIONS FOR COMMUNITY COLLEGES (ISSN 0194-3081, electronic ISSN 1536-0733) is part of The Jossey-Bass Higher and Adult Education Series and is published quarterly by Wiley Subscription Services, Inc., A Wiley Company, at Jossey-Bass, 989 Market Street, San Francisco, California 94103-1741. Periodicals Postage Paid at San Francisco, California, and at additional mailing offices. POSTMASTER: Send address changes to New Directions for Community Colleges, Jossey-Bass, 989 Market Street, San Francisco, California 94103-1741.

SUBSCRIPTIONS cost $89.00 for individuals and $228.00 for institutions, agencies, and libraries in the United States. Prices subject to change. See order form at the back of book.

EDITORIAL CORRESPONDENCE should be sent to the Editor-in-Chief, Arthur M. Cohen, at the Graduate School of Education and Information Studies, University of California, Box 951521, Los Angeles, California 90095-1521. All manuscripts receive anonymous reviews by external referees.

New Directions for Community Colleges is indexed in CIJE: Current Index to Journals in Education (ERIC), Contents Pages in Education (T&F), Current Abstracts (EBSCO), Ed/Net (Simpson Communications), Education Index/Abstracts (H. W. Wilson), Educational Research Abstracts Online (T&F), ERIC Database (Education Resources Information Center), and Resources in Education (ERIC).

Microfilm copies of issues and articles are available in 16mm and 35mm, as well as microfiche in 105mm, through University Microfilms Inc., 300 North Zeeb Road, Ann Arbor, Michigan 48106-1346.

Contents

EDITOR'S NOTES
Trudy H. Bers
1

1. Using Transcripts in Analyses: Directions and Opportunities
Linda Serra Hagedorn, Anne M. Kress
Practical lessons about how to do transcript analyses and to track student progress through transcript data are described in this chapter.
7

2. Retention Tracking Using Institutional Data
Fred Lillibridge
In this chapter, the author explains a sophisticated approach for tracking student cohorts within an institution, from entry through departure.
19

3. Using Student Tracking Data from an Institutional Perspective
Joanne Bashford
This chapter describes several examples of institutional use of state- and college-level tracking data to benchmark performance, improve student success, and enhance program effectiveness.
31

4. A Statewide Student Unit Record System: Florida as a Case Study
Jay Pfeiffer, Patricia Windham
The chapter describes the evolution, content, and use of Florida's unit record system, which includes K–16 and employment data. It includes examples of how information derived from tracking is used both for state-level policy making and institution-level research and practice.
37

5. The National Student Clearinghouse: The Largest Current Student Tracking Database
Craig Schoenecker, Richard Reeves
The authors describe the National Student Clearinghouse, and opportunities and challenges for tracking community college students. They also offer system and institutional perspectives on using clearinghouse data to supply more comprehensive student and graduate tracking for reporting and accountability.
47

6. Tracking Low-Skill Adult Students Longitudinally: Using 59
Research to Guide Policy and Practice
David Prince
Important constituencies for community colleges, noncredit and workforce development students are often ignored when institutions track
students and report on outcomes. The author explores how the state
of Washington examines the progress, performance, and outcomes of
noncredit and workforce development students and also notes special
challenges in researching these populations.

7. Using State Student Unit Record Data to Increase 71
Community College Student Success
Peter Ewell, Davis Jenkins
This chapter builds on a recent eleven state audit of student unit sys-
tems and subsequent work describing such systems and their utility for
policy makers.

8. Beyond Higher Education: Other Sources of Data for 83
Tracking Students
David Stevens
A variety of nationwide systems might be used for tracking students;
one example is the federal Employment Data Exchange System, which
offers access to a variety of resources.

9. Conclusion and the Future 93
Trudy H. Bers
This brief concluding chapter presents final observations about track-
ing community college students.

INDEX 97

EDITOR'S NOTES

Nearly twenty years ago, I edited an issue of *New Directions for Community Colleges* that focused on student tracking. A number of articles in that issue concentrated on how student tracking was being used, or could be used, to identify and communicate with prospective students, students in academic difficulty, and students making their way through an institution. Now, student tracking is of even greater interest. But there has been a shift in focus. There is less interest in prospective students and students in academic difficulty, and more in understanding student progress through and beyond a single college or university. This new emphasis comes from a variety of sources, among them state and public calls for accountability, accreditation criteria placing more attention on learning outcomes, and increased awareness that many students swirl through multiple institutions as they move from initial entry in postsecondary education to completion of an undergraduate degree or final dropout. At the same time, National Center for Education Statistics (NCES) longitudinal datasets such as the Baccalaureate and Beyond, Beginning Postsecondary Students, and High School and Beyond are giving researchers the tools to document and create wider awareness of transfer and swirling behaviors. These are critical resources, but they do not help institutions know about their own students.

Another powerful driver is recognition by colleges that enrollment alone is not necessarily tantamount to success. No longer satisfied with offering only access, community colleges are now focused on students' success. Many indicators of success, discussed in subsequent chapters, require tracking students both during their tenure within an institution and after they leave it.

The shift to understanding student success is accompanied by a related change: using data from student tracking to (1) measure institutional or programmatic effectiveness and (2) employ tracking results to identify how effectiveness might be improved. In other words, tracking results are being used to help the institution improve, not just to increase individual students' success.

In addition, legal, organizational, and technical changes have prompted more interest in tracking students and at the same time greater ability and more concerns about doing so. What are some of the key changes? The Higher Education Act requires colleges to report the graduation rate of first-time, full-time students, using a three-year timetable for community colleges, and the transfer-out rate for the same cohort. The National Student Clearinghouse, which did not exist twenty years ago, now has student unit

records for more than 90 percent of students enrolled in higher education. Similarly, state student unit record (SUR) systems were in their infancy. Now, more than forty states have such systems, although many include just public institutions or do not link with K–12 or other systems. At the state level, there is much activity in linking state higher education data with data from other sources, such as unemployment insurance (UI) wage records, to gain a fuller understanding of what happens to students and alumni in the labor market. National initiatives such as Achieving the Dream require or strongly encourage participating institutions to track cohorts of students from entry through graduation, transfer, or dropout.

From a technical perspective, electronic capacity to store and link datasets has expanded exponentially in the past twenty years. Relational databases, query tools, graphic data displays, and electronic transfer of data are among the tools we now take for granted. Together, they make it possible for institutional researchers and others to compile, manipulate, display, and share large amounts of student data while still preserving individual student anonymity. Although technology has made tracking more feasible, human intervention is still required to ensure data security, maintain compliance with operational definitions of variables, clean data, and monitor creation and use of datasets.

Because student tracking continues to be a topic of great interest and importance, and because so much has changed in the last years, I proposed a new issue of *New Directions for Community Colleges*, again focused on student tracking. The authors who accepted my invitation to participate in this issue have great experience in building, maintaining, understanding, and using data systems that permit us to identify and then follow students across time, within and between institutions, and into the world of work. More important, they recognize that tracking students is not an end in itself but a vehicle for understanding how students navigate postsecondary education, and for gauging and measuring student success.

A common theme threading together these chapters, one not prescribed at the outset of this project, is reliance on quantitative data at the student and employee level as the core building block on which the ability to track students rests. I shall return to the subject of student unit records in my concluding chapter. Suffice it to say here that other approaches for tracking students, such as conducting surveys to elicit self-reported data from current and former students or contacting employers to learn about graduates employed in their businesses, did not receive much attention from chapter authors. Although important methods for learning about student outcomes and success, they do not appear brightly on the radar screen of those who engage in tracking students.

This issue is organized from the particular to the general, from looking at the course-level work of individual students to understanding employment patterns in broadly defined geographic regions, within and across industries, and among populations defined by characteristics such as age and gender.

Linda Serra Hagedorn and Anne Kress draw from the Transfer and Retention of Urban Community College Students (TRUCCS) Project to present examples of how transcript analyses yield insights into how students attend college, enroll in courses, and achieve—or do not achieve—success. They assert that using transcripts gives researchers data about actual student behavior, data not degraded by poor memory or a desire to tell a story different from reality. Hagedorn and Kress also offer concrete instructions to enable researchers to conduct similar analyses at their home institutions. Their work demonstrates the rich analyses possible with data to which most institutions have ready access, if not the skilled personnel to compile and present the data meaningfully.

In his chapter about tracking cohorts through an institution, Fred Lillibridge demonstrates how researchers can compile data on students' progress through an institution term-by-term, including stop-out semesters, and into other institutions. Focusing primarily on responding to the federal government's required reporting of graduation and retention rates, Lillibridge's model permits investigation of cohort patterns by race and ethnicity, gender, age, or other variables captured in the student information system. His approach differs from the Hagedorn and Kress model; they look at students' course-taking patterns and attainments, while Lillibridge concentrates on the more global variables of semester enrollment and degree and certificate completion.

Joanne Bashford's chapter describes several examples of institutional use of state- and college-level tracking data to benchmark performance, improve student success, and enhance program effectiveness. Miami Dade College is located in Florida, a state with one of the most comprehensive SUR data files. She illustrates how an institution can make excellent use of state and local data to examine the progress and performance of its own students. In particular, the author shows how comparing Miami Dade's data with statewide data yielded a framework to help the institution better understand its own students. Bashford's chapter also illustrates how qualitative research can complement and enrich understanding of student performance in ways that quantitative data alone cannot.

Moving from the institutional to the state level, the chapter written by Jay Pfeiffer and Patricia Windham describes the evolution, content, and use of Florida's unit record system, which includes K–16 and employment data. As just noted, the Florida system is widely regarded as one of the most mature and comprehensive student systems and permits tracking in ways that other state systems cannot support. Chapter Four includes examples of how information derived from tracking is used for state-level, state-agency-level, and institution-level research and practice. Together, Chapters Four and Five furnish an excellent perspective on the benefits of student tracking for different constituencies.

In Chapter Five, Craig Schoenecker and Richard Reeves present a description of the National Student Clearinghouse, which now includes enrollment data from more than three thousand postsecondary education institutions, representing approximately 92 percent of the nation's postsecondary students. They give sufficient information about the Clearinghouse's StudentTracker program to enable readers to understand how it works and make a preliminary assessment of whether their institution can benefit from joining, especially supplying degree information to augment enrollment information. Using data from Minnesota and neighboring states, Schoenecker and Reeves illustrate how clearinghouse data show higher transfer numbers than state systems alone, and the interstate movement of students to and from Minnesota.

In his chapter, David Prince describes how the Washington State Board for Community and Technical Colleges used the findings from a tracking study for low-skill, working-age adults to significantly influence and change state policy and practice for this critical component of the state's workforce. He summarizes results of a number of studies. One of them found a substantial difference in earnings between students who completed one year or more of college plus a credential and those who did not make it to that tipping point. In another study, the board looked at results of the Integrated Basic Education and Skills Training (I-BEST) program. I-BEST pairs English as a second language (ESL) or adult basic education (ABE) and professional-technical instructors in the classroom to concurrently plan curricula, instruction, and shared learning outcomes. Results from the pilot programs demonstrated that I-BEST students were substantially more likely to earn college credits and complete training than were traditional ESL students during the same time period.

In Chapter Seven, Peter Ewell and Davis Jenkins present results of a recent eleven-state audit of SUR systems. They identify key lessons learned about creation and use of these systems, as well as barriers to and suggestions for strengthening the use of SUR data. In a rich exhibit, they suggest narrative story lines and research questions that illustrate how SUR data can be used to explore questions of priority to a state.

David Stevens's chapter brings a new dimension to understanding student tracking. He describes the Federal Employment Data Exchange System (FEDES), which permits determining a current or former student's status as a federal employee, and three new Census Bureau tools that deliver user-defined insights about geographic, demographic, and economic target markets. The FEDES supplements UI wage records, which do not contain data on federal employment. The first of the Census Bureau tools is the Quarterly Workforce Indicators Online, which includes eight employment indicators such as new hires, average hire earnings, and job creation, with each available for substate regions, age, gender, and North American Industry Classification System (NAICS) code. The second is the Industry Focus Tool, which ranks data on a variety of variables such as number of new hires or average hire earnings, again by user-defined subgroups such as age or substate regions. The third tool is On the Map, which depicts employment location for area residents or, conversely, employment within an area by residence of the employee. The chapter includes exhibits that illustrate results using the three tools.

In my concluding chapter, I offer observations about the current state of student tracking in community colleges.

Trudy H. Bers
Editor

TRUDY H. BERS is executive director of research, curriculum, and planning at Oakton Community College.

1

This chapter offers practical lessons about the research methodology of transcript analysis and details the benefits and usefulness of tracking student progress through transcript data.

Using Transcripts in Analyses: Directions and Opportunities

Linda Serra Hagedorn, Anne M. Kress

Recently, community colleges have faced escalating and intense drives to appropriately use data in decision-making processes. Terms such as "culture of evidence" and "evidence-based decisions" have not only crept into discussions at many community colleges but are becoming institutional buzzwords. Juxtaposed with the quest for evidence has been the lament that community colleges have insufficient databases or have been lax in uniform collection of data. In this chapter, we take issue with the accusations that community colleges exist in nondata-rich environments. On the contrary, we argue that all community colleges have a wealth of data that are currently used for multiple purposes. Further, these existing data have great potential for understanding community college students' success if coded, defined, and subjected to analysis. In the pages that follow, we discuss the art and practice of transcript analysis as well as offer ideas and examples of measures that can be derived from enrollment data.

We define transcript analysis as the coding and use of enrollment files, college application data, financial aid records, and other data that community colleges must routinely collect to comply with state and federal reporting mandates. Although the format and structure of data may vary from institution to institution, all accredited postsecondary institutions must keep records of the courses students take, the grades they earn, and the degrees they receive. These records have an untapped potential for promoting policies to help students succeed.

NEW DIRECTIONS FOR COMMUNITY COLLEGES, no. 143, Fall 2008 © 2008 Wiley Periodicals, Inc.
Published online in Wiley InterScience (www.interscience.wiley.com) • DOI: 10.1002/cc.331

The root of most transcript-analysis-based research is Clifford Adelman's work with the U.S. Department of Education. Adelman (1999, 2004, 2005, 2006) has published a series of now-canonical studies based on longitudinal transcript research. In a recent interview, Adelman indicated, "Transcripts don't lie, exaggerate, by-pass or forget, but people responding to surveys do all of the above" (Burd, 2004, para. 22). This sense of transcripts as a more objective data source has driven acceptance of Adelman's research findings within higher education. Another compelling aspect of transcript analysis is the ability of the researcher to track what Adelman (2006) calls the academic momentum of students: complex movement patterns through the curriculum that could be forward, backward, static, or all three together in any one term.

Community colleges seem to offer a particularly apt environment for transcript analysis because their students engage with an institution primarily in the classroom (Borglum and Kubala, 2000). The only trace of the presence of some community college students is found in their transcripts. Thus it is reasonable to conclude that transcript records offer a prime marker of student engagement. Transcripts answer many simple and complex questions: How long did the student attend the college? Was the enrollment continuous or sporadic? Was the enrollment full- or part-time? Was there a pattern of dropping courses? What was the level of academic success?

Transcripts also offer a map of the curriculum as traveled by the student. Extending the analogy, transcripts serve as a guide to fast roads, slow roads, danger spots, and insurmountable barriers. They also furnish detail on the timetable of the journey to degree. For all these reasons, transcript analysis has yielded rich portraits of students' experiences at their educational institution (Adelman, 2006; Calcagno, Crosta, Bailey, and Jenkins, 2006; Hagedorn and others, 2006; Jenkins, 2006; Windham, 2006).

As a methodology, transcript analysis has been employed productively in higher education to help shape policy and practice. One of the largest states, Florida, has adopted this research framework as the foundation for its own system-wide, longitudinal community college data warehouse. Moreover, researchers have found transcript analysis useful for studies with a much tighter focus. For example, Lucas and Mott (1996) relied on this methodology to identify the efficacy of learning communities. Patthey-Chavez, Thomas-Spiegel, and Dillon (1998) used transcript analysis in their study concerning the success of students in remedial writing courses. By focusing on the transcript, a researcher can read a student's academic history, her or his momentum through college, the academic resources she or he builds during studies, as well as whether resources (especially time) were used wisely or squandered. The transcript also reveals whether students entered into the postsecondary system with a deficit in academic capital that might have placed them well behind their peers.

The TRUCCS Project

To explain how transcript analysis may be used to analyze community college student success, we use data and examples from the Transfer and Retention of Urban Community College Students (TRUCCS) Project. The TRUCCS Project began with administration of a survey during the spring of 2001. The survey was designed by a team of researchers from the University of Southern California, the Los Angeles Community College District, and the University of California at Los Angeles. A questionnaire specifically designed for urban community college students was administered to 5,011 students across 241 classrooms in nine colleges within the district. Along with the questionnaire, students agreed to open their college records (enrollment data, financial data, and other college records) for the purposes of the stated research. Though the demographic, psychosocial, and satisfaction data collected by the surveys were informative and highly useful to the research project, the researchers quickly discovered that the real value of the project was the ability to analyze college records.

Transcript Analysis

Although transcript analysis can be complex and include a range of analyses and approaches, we decided to give two examples of transcript analysis as a means of explaining the process and its nuances. We also discuss the process of collecting transcript stories as an alternate but powerful means through their transcript records. The first example of transcript analysis illustrates an easy progression; the second offers guidance through a more complex process.

The Enrollment File. Figure 1.1 presents a fictitious example of a transcript or enrollment file using enrollment as the unit of analysis (each line represents an enrollment in one course). Although college files and databases likely have additional information, most college files include these data fields:

- Identification number (ID): the ID could be a social security number, a college assigned number, or another designator, but each student must have a unique identifier code. Each line of enrollment data represents a registration for a course. For each ID number, there is a one-to-one correspondence between the number of lines of data and the number of courses in which the student is enrolled.
- Campus designator: multicampus colleges will require a designator for the campus.
- Semester: this term refers to the semester in which the enrollment occurred. The template uses a popular designation where the first four digits are the year and the last digit designates a semester (1 = spring; 2 = summer; 3 = fall). Thus the designation 20001 indicates the spring semester of the year 2000.

NEW DIRECTIONS FOR COMMUNITY COLLEGES • DOI: 10.1002/cc

Figure 1.1. Sample Enrollment File in SPSS

	id	campu	sem	add	drop	subabrv	number	section	grade	units
1	909816	Main	19983	08/11/03	.	ENGLISH	50	285	P	3.00
2	909816	Main	19993	09/05/99		CO SCI	101	276	A	3.00
3	909816	Main	20061	01/01/01	01/12/01	AUTO	100	788		.00
4	968466	North	19953	06/30/95	11/06/95	MATH	100	221	W	.00
5	1133447	Main	19993	07/30/99	08/17/99	MATH	110	503		.00
6	1133447	Main	20063	06/05/03	.	SPEECH	101	291	B	3.00
7	1133447	East	20061	11/29/04	.	ENGLISH	101	374	A	3.00
8	1234565	South	19951	12/05/04	01/13/04	ENGLISH	101	127		.00
9	1234565	South	19993	08/16/01	08/30/01	TUTOR	1	977		.00
10	1234565	South	20061	02/08/01		CO SCI	102	263	A	3.00
11	1994858	Main	20001	11/29/00	01/24/00	COMMUN	15	818		.00
12	1994858	Main	20063	05/12/03	08/15/03	ECON	101	197		.00
13	2765598	West	19993	08/02/99	11/20/99	EARTH	101	370	W	.00
14	2785943	West	20001	01/12/00	.	ECON	101	865	C	3.00
15	3654048	North	20063	07/03/03	.	POL SCI	101	307	B	3.00

- Add date: the exact date the student added the course to his or her schedule.
- Drop date: the date the student dropped the course, if applicable.
- Department: this field refers to the department designation of the course. For example, ENG denotes all courses in the English Department.
- Course number: if the department is ENG, the number 101 in this category would signify the course English 101.
- Section number: typically colleges offer many sections of the same course. The section number can be useful when investigating issues pertaining to a specific instructor, the time or day of the week the section was offered, or the enrollment in that section.
- Grade: this field refers to the grade the student earned. In our example, blanks indicate the course was dropped prior to census date.
- Units: this refers to the number of units of course credit supplied by the course.

Example One: Course Completion Ratio. For an initial example of transcript analysis, we present the case of the course completion ratio (CCR). The CCR is an important measure of retention for community colleges. Simply put, the course completion ratio is the proportion of enrolled courses that a student completes. This simple measure is of utmost importance in understanding student success given that course completion is the basic building block of community college accomplishment. A student cannot graduate, transfer, or earn a certificate without passing the courses within the program of study. Because the reference is the student's enrollment in courses, the measure gauges success against the student's stated goals. Even though the value and validity of grades may be challenged, higher education continues to use grades as evidence of learning and accomplishment. CCR is a simple yet strong measure with a more sensitive range of variation than the typical dichotomous measure of retention used in many studies (Hagedorn, 2004a; Hagedorn and others, 2006).

Transcript analysis is an application and practice in logic. We find it useful to first identify what we are trying to measure, then identify the factors or variables needed to create the measure, and finally process extraction from the enrollment data files. The CCR is operationalized as the quotient of the number of courses (alternatively, one could substitute the number of credits) successfully completed (grade of A, B, or C; P in the case of classes graded with a pass-no pass scale) divided by the number of courses attempted. Note that the researcher defines the time span (one semester, one year, or five years).

$$CCR = \frac{\text{Number of courses with grade of A, B, C, or P}}{\text{Number of courses of enrollment}}$$

Figure 1.2 gives a picture of the resulting file with the CCR calculated for each student (note that the unit of analysis has now shifted from enrollment to the student). The example presents only a basic CCR calculation. With minor modifications limiting the data to a specific time period or discipline, a specific or more focused CCR can be calculated with a few added steps.

Example Two: The Developmental Climb. The TRUCCS project defined *developmental climb* as the progression through the various levels of developmental or remedial courses to transfer level. For example, a student in remedial mathematics may need to take two courses (Introduction to Algebra and Intermediate Algebra) before enrollment in a transfer-level course (College Algebra). Studying the developmental climb included the measures of grades earned, the number of times each course was attempted, and the number of semesters between steps (Hagedorn, 2004b).

In this second example of transcript analysis, we show a paradigm where the enrollment begins as the unit of analysis but the outcome of interest is a cohort or campus measure. Specifically, we examine the pass rate

Figure 1.2. SPSS File with Calculated Course Completion Ratio

	id	attempt_sum	pass_sum	CCR
1	282167077	2.00	2.00	1.00
2	300356578	1.00	.00	.00
3	351523194	2.00	2.00	1.00
4	382883569	1.00	1.00	1.00
5	618678118	.	.	.
6	857712662	1.00	.00	.00
7	864022387	1.00	1.00	1.00
8	1133253364	1.00	1.00	1.00
9	1196712858	1.00	1.00	1.00

among the various levels of developmental mathematics. Table 1.1 gives the fold logic and step syntax of the developmental climb through a math curriculum structure consisting of four levels, where level three is transfer-level math, level two is a prerequisite for level three, level one is a prerequisite for level two, and level zero is the lowest level offered. The climb begins with a group of students who initially were placed (via district placement testing) in level zero. The outcome of interest is a trace of the cohort proportions that successfully complete a level zero mathematics course, enroll in a level one course, pass the level one course, enroll in a level two course, and so on.

Additional Uses of Transcript Analysis

The two previous examples offer evidence that transcript analysis can be used to analyze groups of students and their academic behaviors. Researchers can also examine individual student-level transcripts to learn more about how students are or are not moving through the curriculum. This type of analysis can be likened to a qualitative in-depth analysis. Examining the individual records reveals transcript stories that often tell narratives of incredible persistence on the part of students.

For example, the transcript in Table 1.2 belongs to an underprepared, traditional-age male student. It has been stripped of all courses beyond those associated with reading, writing, and mathematics, both to ensure student anonymity and to focus on the academic core. This first-time college student placed into remedial work in all three foundational subject areas: writing, math, and reading. In his first term, he attempted all three course areas but was successful in just one (reading). In his second term, he scaled back his enrollment, focusing on his one area of success and one of his two weaker areas. Again, he was successful only in reading. Then, like many traditional students, he stopped out over summer. Given his lack of preparation, this decision is likely to be counterproductive because it interrupts his immersion into the academic environment, and indeed the transcript bears out this supposition. He enrolled for only one course in the following fall and was unsuccessful. Still, he persisted into spring and finally succeeded in completing developmental writing a full *two years* after beginning his journey in this *one course*. In the case of this student, looking closely at the narrative of the transcript suggests that, although underprepared for college academically, he had an incredible drive to succeed.

This transcript also presents compelling evidence of the barrier that math courses present for many college students. Although this student kept striving to succeed in writing, he essentially dropped math as a viable subject after his first term and did not return to this subject until a full two years later. Thus the transcript offers nuance to the math-barrier discussion: math avoidance. Although he was successful in his retake of Developmental Math 1, the student failed Developmental Math 2 and stopped out. When

Table 1.1. Logic and Step of the Developmental Climb

Logic	Step
Part 1: Developing the Data File	
Create a file containing only math enrollments.	Select only math enrollments.
Assign math levels.	Determine the steps. Assign lowest level as 0. Continue through transfer level. Note in this example level 0 is a prerequisite for level 1, level 1 is a prerequisite for level 2, and so on.
Mark all enrollments.	Create a variable to mark the enrollments. Note an enrollment is separate from a "pass." This variable will be needed to determine the levels of math in which the student enrolled.
Determine courses that were successfully completed.	Code grades of A, B, C, D, or P as passed. Create a dichotomous variable of passed (1) or not passed (0).
Save the resulting file for future use.	Save the file using the name math enroll.
Create a file that is aggregated by student ID that sums the number of enrollments by math level and the number of passes by math level.	The aggregate command creates new variables, such as the sum, mean, and other measures of the original file variables. Aggregate by ID and math level. Create a sum variable for enrollments and passes.
Determine the proportion of courses passed in each level.	For this analysis the researcher is not interested in the number of courses passed, but rather if any at that level were passed. Therefore a new variable that records any pass must be calculated. Split the file by math level. Calculate the proportion of passes. Because the variable pass is dichotomous, the mean will provide the proportion of courses passed.
Part 2: Determining the Proportion of Students Who Passed Level 0 and Enrolled in Level 1	
For this analysis, we begin a longitudinal approach and are interested in those who passed a level 0.	Continue to use enroll and pass dataset.
Identify those who have enrolled in a math level 1 course.	Select only levels 0 and 1. Identify those students who enrolled in level 1. A new variable called enroll1 will be created. Note the lag command checks for the same ID number in two rows.
Part 3: Determining the Proportion of Students Who Enrolled in Level 1 and Passed	
Determine the proportion of those who enrolled in level 1 and passed it.	Create a new variable that marks passing of level 1 courses. From the longitudinal angle, determine those who enrolled in level 1 and passed.

NEW DIRECTIONS FOR COMMUNITY COLLEGES • DOI: 10.1002/cc

Table 1.2. Sample Student Transcript

Course	Grade	Term	Year
Developmental Writing 2	F	Fall	2000
Developmental Writing Lab 2	F	Fall	2000
Developmental Math 1	F	Fall	2000
Developmental Math Lab 1	F	Fall	2000
Developmental Reading 2	C	Fall	2000
Developmental Reading Lab 2	C	Fall	2000
Developmental Writing 2	D	Spring	2001
Developmental Writing Lab 2	D	Spring	2001
College Reading	C	Spring	2001
Developmental Writing 2	D	Fall	2001
Developmental Writing Lab 2	D	Fall	2001
Developmental Writing 2	B	Spring	2002
Developmental Writing Lab 2	C+	Spring	2002
Developmental Math 1	C	Fall	2002
Developmental Math Lab 1	C	Fall	2002
College Composition	D+	Fall	2002
College Composition	W	Spring	2003
Developmental Math 2	F	Spring	2003
Developmental Math 2	F	Fall	2003
Developmental Math 2	F	Spring	2005

he returned a year later, he was again unsuccessful and again stopped, or possibly even dropped out. Our student becomes yet another example of the critical role math plays in college retention and success. His repeated failures in the subject bring an end to his college journey.

In addition to revealing his personal enrollment narrative, the student's transcript also suggests a larger research question regarding the transition between courses. Twice he earned a passing grade in one level of a subject but was unsuccessful in his attempt at the next level. This situation may be an anomaly, but it also suggests that the transition between courses is far rockier than expected. Transcript analysis on a larger sample of students could supply data on the rate of first-time success experienced by students as they move from level to level in any academic area. If students were routinely unsuccessful as they moved from remedial to college writing, faculty might find and correct disconnects between the two courses that have a negative impact for students.

Looking in detail at this student's story is also important because it peeks below the surface of aggregate data on success and failure. Our student came to college woefully unprepared but continued to push forward for more than three years trying to make up for his academic deficiencies before finally giving up. His persistence deserves recognition and suggests a student desperate for academic intervention. However, these narratives

NEW DIRECTIONS FOR COMMUNITY COLLEGES • DOI: 10.1002/cc

often get lost in the avalanche of data. As we mine our institutional records, we should not lose sight of the students behind them. Analyzing the transcript data at any single college, we would find many similar stories of evidence for how students need—and deserve—support in their academic quest. Because we serve individual students, their individual journeys are important.

Overcoming Limitations

Though it has incredible power as a research tool, transcript analysis does have limitations. Transcripts give essential information on the *what* of the curriculum and the *how* of students' movement through that curriculum. However, they do not, in and of themselves, reveal "*why*" students make the choices or earn the grades they do. To answer these questions, researchers need to gather additional information. The survey administered to students in the TRUCCS project has enabled the researchers to look at the complex nexus of academic, social, cultural, and even financial issues that manifest themselves in the student transcript records.

Colleges interested in creating a useful framework for research might consider supplementing transcript analysis with nationally normed survey data such as the Community College Survey of Student Engagement, their own exit or course satisfaction surveys, or focus group discussions to illuminate the reasons behind student choices. In some cases, researchers using student satisfaction or attitudinal surveys can link the resulting data to transcript data through student identifiers, creating significant data mining opportunities. Colleges opting to enhance their understanding of student record data with focus group or individual student interviews gain a general sense of students' own explanations for their behaviors. As Tinto's research (2007) has shown, students' language choices frequently reveal much more than they might realize and can prove quite enlightening about their motivations. Any of these strategies will enhance the power of transcript analysis, adding dimensions and depth.

Conclusion

As they seek to build cultures of inquiry and evidence, community colleges have access to extraordinarily powerful information about their students already embedded in the transcript record. Unfortunately this rich vein frequently goes undermined, or not mined at all. As the TRUCCS study and others have demonstrated, there is great value in transcript-based research. Such projects give a more meaningful context for meaningful discussion and action on the topic of community college student retention, completion, and transfer (Hagedorn, 2005; Hagedorn, Maxwell, and Moon, 2001) and offer a firm foundation for further research into student behaviors and motivations. As community college professionals know all too well, demands for accountability seem to be escalating even as the resources for meeting these demands are diminishing. Thus it seems imperative that community colleges become more active in making the most effective and efficient use of data readily available in their student record systems. As the body of transcript analysis-based research grows, it will help illuminate and explain the complex and sometimes vexing paths community college students take on their trek through higher education.

References

Adelman, C. *Answers in the Tool Box: Academic Intensity, Attendance Patterns, and Bachelor's Degree Attainment.* Washington, D.C.: U.S. Department of Education, 1999.

Adelman, C. *Principal Indicators of Student Academic Histories in Postsecondary Education: 1972–2000.* Washington, D.C.: U.S. Department of Education, 2004.

Adelman, C. *Moving into Town and Moving On: The Community College in the Lives of Traditional-Age Students.* Washington, D.C.: U.S. Department of Education, 2005.

Adelman, C. *The Toolbox Revisited: Paths to Degree Completion from High School Through College.* Washington, D.C.: U.S. Department of Education, 2006.

Borglum, K., and Kubala, T. "Academic and Social Integration of Community College Students: A Case Study." *Community College Journal of Research and Practice,* 2000, 24(7), 567–576.

Burd, S. "Misgauging College Performance With Graduation Rates?" Washington, D.C.: *Chronicle of Higher Education,* 2004. Podcast. http://chronicle.com/colloquylive/2004/04/rates/ (accessed May 20, 2008).

Calcagno, J., Crosta, P., Bailey, T., and Jenkins, D. *Stepping Stones to a Degree: The Impact of Enrollment Pathways and Milestones on Community College Student* Outcomes. New York: Community College Research Center, Teachers College, Columbia University, 2006.

Hagedorn, L. S. "How to Define Retention: A New Look at an Old Problem." In A. Seidman (ed.), *College Student Retention: Formula for Student Success.* Westport, Conn.: Greenwood, 2004a.

Hagedorn, L. S. *Speaking Community College: A Glossary of Appropriate Terms.* Los Angeles: Rossier School of Education, University of Southern California, 2004b. http://www.coe.ufl.edu/Leadership/ihe/TRUCCS/Files/Speaking_Community_College.pdf (accessed May 20, 2008).

Hagedorn, L. S. "Transcript Analyses as a Tool to Understand Community College Student Academic Behaviors." *Journal of Applied Research in the Community College,* 2005, 13(1), 45–57.

Hagedorn, L. S., Maxwell, W. E., and Moon, H. S. "Research on Urban Community College Transfer and Retention." Los Angeles: Rossier School of Education, University of Southern California, 2001. http://www.truccs.org (accessed May 22, 2008).

Hagedorn, L. S., and others. "Transfer Between Community Colleges and Four-Year Colleges: The All-American Game." *Community College Journal of Research and Practice,* 2006, 30(3), 223–242.

Jenkins, D. *What Community College Management Practices Are Effective in Promoting Student Success? A Study of High- and Low-Impact Institutions.* New York: Community College Research Center, Teachers College, Columbia University, 2006.

Lucas, J. A., and Mott, J. *Learning Communities' Impact on National Agenda Goals for Higher Education.* Palatine, Ill.: William Rainey Harper College, 1996.

Patthey-Chavez, G. G., Thomas-Spiegel, J., and Dillon, P. *Tracking Outcomes for Community College Students with Different Writing Instruction Histories.* Los Angeles: Los Angeles City College, 1998.

Tinto, V. "Promoting the Success of Academically Under-Prepared Students." Paper presented at the Community College Survey of Student Engagement Annual Workshop, Austin, Tex., May 2007.

Windham, P. *Impact of Withdrawing from Courses Revisited.* Tallahassee: Florida Department of Education, 2006.

LINDA SERRA HAGEDORN is professor and director of the Research Institute for Studies in Education (RISE) at Iowa State University in Ames, Iowa.

ANNE M. KRESS is provost and vice president for academic affairs at Santa Fe Community College in Gainesville, Florida.

2

This chapter presents a sophisticated approach for track-
ing student cohorts from entry through departure within
an institution. It describes how a researcher can create a
student tracking model to perform longitudinal research
on student cohorts.

Retention Tracking Using Institutional Data

Fred Lillibridge

Longitudinal research is the collection and analysis of data at discrete time intervals over a period of time. The model described in this chapter was developed by an institutional research (IR) office to track students by semester in order to explore what happened over time to students who entered the college during a specific semester. These students make up a cohort, defined as a group of students who meet a set of common conditions. Did they persist, stop out, transfer, graduate, or drop out of college?

The model was developed to produce the data necessary to complete the Integrated Postsecondary Education Data System (IPEDS) Graduation Rate Survey (GRS) in compliance with the Student Right-to-Know and Campus Security Act of 1990. The act requires postsecondary education entities that receive Title IV financial aid funds to compile and release the institutionwide graduation rate to all students. Typical retention rates are fall to spring, fall to fall, and fall to fall to fall. Completion rates are produced for entering cohorts after three years and beyond.

Notice the model for complying with the GRS focuses on enrollment and certificate and degree completion. It does not delve into questions related to course-taking patterns, movement through remedial to college-level coursework, course completion ratios, grade point averages, or other measures of academic success. In contrast to the rich findings possible through transcript analysis, tracking the enrollment and completion of student cohorts yields information at the macro level of an institution.

NEW DIRECTIONS FOR COMMUNITY COLLEGES, no. 143, Fall 2008 © 2008 Wiley Periodicals, Inc.
Published online in Wiley InterScience (www.interscience.wiley.com) • DOI: 10.1002/cc.332

The specific approach to longitudinal research presented in this chapter allows the researcher to measure student flow, persistence, and completion over time. The model is used to calculate a variety of retention and completion rates, and it allows the researcher to show results by incorporating the model in a supplemental spreadsheet.

Start with Data

Gaining access to institutional data is the first step of the research process. Institutional researchers will likely discover that other campus units control the data they need. Establishing an effective relationship with the data custodians is essential to success. The information technology unit and IR office often do not look at data in the same way. Most transactional data systems are designed to support essential college operations and not to supply data for IR offices.

The IR office needs to establish a consistent procedure to extract data from the student information system and store it on a secure computer or server. At a minimum, this needs to be done at two critical times during each semester: on the official census date and following the end of the semester after grades are posted. Generally these files are called the census and final files. Together they can be used to establish a basic data warehouse.

Institutional researchers also need to develop procedures to make sure the extracted data are accurate. Data must be cleaned by examining data anomalies and working with student services offices and other data custodians to correct miscodes and find and enter missing data. Decisions must be made about what data should be updated. It is usually necessary to update student ID numbers that may have changed or been corrected because a student's unique identification code serves as the key variable used to join or link his or her records from different data files. Many researchers also find it useful to update grades that may have changed after the final file was created.

Anyone conducting or evaluating longitudinal studies should be aware that no student information system is perfect. Data errors result from mistakes in data entry and incorrect data supplied by students. Also, students behave in ways that are inconsistent with our textbook descriptions of enrollment. For example, students may sit in on classes but not register until later in the term or even after the semester ends. They may register for multiple sections of the same course during the same semester or register for lower-level prerequisites after completing the higher-level course in a sequence. Researchers must weigh the costs of pursuing and achieving data perfection against the benefits, taking into consideration how and by whom the data will be used and the impact of using imperfect data.

Next, the data files need to be frozen so that changes can no longer be made. The decision about when to extract and then freeze the data is up to the researcher. It is important to do this so that research findings will hit the same data over time and produce consistent results. It is not unusual to delay the final freeze for a year or more. The IR office should then secure the data files so that unauthorized individuals cannot access them. Data files also need to be backed up early and often. It is important that copies of the data files be put in a safe place other than the location where the data warehouse is stored so that a single disaster will not destroy both sets of files.

Data Files

This model relies on a series of flat files that contain text or ASCII data in a fixed field format. This approach offers several advantages. Flat files make it possible for the researcher to use the files with all types of software (SAS, SPSS, Access, Excel). Most researchers have preferences about which software tools they want to use. This approach has an added advantage in allowing researchers to use many tools to access the data files and permitting adaptation to future software changes. The IR office should have access to text editor software to edit these large files.

The longitudinal model relies on several basic files created from internal data sources. Virtually all institutions have these data, although the ease of accessing them varies. Each record in a file contains one or more keys that permit joining records from a number of files by matching keys. A key may be a student identification code, a course reference, or another identifier.

Student Demographic File. The most important file is the student demographic file. It contains data elements about individual students that typically come from the admissions and registration system. Individual student records are often referred to as unit record data. There is one record per student, containing variables or data fields such as a student identification code, name, date of birth, sex, race or ethnicity, high school information, major, cumulative GPA, cumulative credit hours, placement test scores, and other available student-specific data. Each variable has one or more values. For example, the variable sex generally has two values, male and female. Because there is just one record per student, the number of these records when totaled is the unduplicated head count for the semester, year, or other time period being examined.

Semester Course File. The semester course file contains information about a student's enrollment during a particular term. A course file is created for the official census date and at the end of the semester. There will be one record per student per enrolled course. The file contains variables such as the term, course prefix, course number, course section, credits, and final grade. Each record has two keys: a student ID and course number. The total of these records will equate to a seat count or the total number of seats occupied by students in all classes. Seat count is a duplicated head count because each student is counted as many times as the number of courses in which he or she is enrolled.

Course Schedule File. This file describes the course being taught and contains variables such as term, instructor information, number of students enrolled, available seats, mode of instruction, and time and location of the course. This file keys on course, which consists of course prefix, number, and section.

Certificate and Degree Completion File. This file contains student completion data, including degrees earned, certificates earned, or any other completions recognized by the college, and the semester the student completed each degree or certificate. The student identification number is the key. The model requires that a degree master file be created. This file contains a single record for each student. Each record shows awarded degrees or certificates for all of the semesters in the certificate and degree completion file. In any semester, a student could have received a certificate, a degree, or neither. If a student is awarded both a certificate and a degree, the value is set to degree because the model considers a degree to be a better outcome than a certificate.

Other Files. Other internal files will add value to the student tracking model if the data are available. Data about financial aid allow researchers to examine differences in persistence and completion by financial aid status. When possible, the IR office should collect data about interventions furnished by the institution. These could include tutor center contacts and activity, advisor contacts, class attendance, and student survey results. To be usable in this model, these data need to be keyed on student ID.

External Transfer Data File. Any student tracking model is enhanced by inclusion of transfer data. Student transfers are considered positive outcomes for community college students. Other institutions, the state higher education office, or the National Student Clearinghouse must supply these files through data sharing agreements. Such agreements must comply with the provisions of the Family Educational Rights and Privacy Act.

Student Tracking Model

The student tracking model example in this chapter measures student outcomes from fall 2004 to spring 2007. The model uses data from fall and spring semesters except for transfer and completion data; degrees and certificates awarded or transfers that occur in summer sessions are coded as the prior spring. Because this model is used to find retention and graduation rates, summer sessions are not deemed critical. Adding summer semesters to the model will increase complexity and reduce the clarity of results. Even though summer sessions are not used in this model, it is important for an IR office to create semester files for summer sessions just as for fall and spring semesters.

Step One: Establish the Cohort. The first step is to determine which students will be in the study cohort. Students included in a particular student tracking cohort must meet a set of common conditions. Because the semester Student Demographic File contains specific student variables, all that is required to create a cohort is to select the desired variables and their values. The most common cohort used in institutional research focuses on new students who did not attend college prior to attending the current institution. The IPEDS Graduation Rate Survey (GRS) for community colleges uses a cohort of first-time, full-time, degree-seeking students as the unit of study. An example of a cohort is all first-time students who were full-time, degree-seeking students in fall 2004. It would be easy to add a filter to select only Hispanic full-time, degree-seeking students or first-time students who took and passed a specific course or courses, such as developmental math. Other examples of cohorts are students entering with a GED, students in a learning community, or any other combination of values found in the Student Demographic File or the Semester Course File.

A cohort file or dataset is created and then merged by student ID with outcomes data to create a longitudinal record by semester for each student in the cohort. The file structures are identical for every semester, so all that is necessary to create a cohort for another semester is to change the name of the file that is being processed; for example, instead of accessing the fall 2004 file the researcher uses the fall 2005 file.

Step Two: Determine Student Outcomes for Each Semester. Using IR data, the researcher can determine these institutional outcomes for each student: a student can persist, stop out (leave for one or more terms and then return), or earn a degree or certificate during any semester. With external files, the researcher can explore whether a student enrolled in another college or university after leaving the home institution. As an aside, it is difficult to track a student who is unknown; an unknown student is defined as one who is not enrolled, did not enroll in any subsequent semesters, or does not appear on any external transfer files. We presume these students have dropped out, but the researcher lacks data to know this with certainty.

The model is intended to lower the number of students with values of unknown by replacing the unknown value with other outcome values. This is primarily done by using transfer and certificate or degree completion data. Determination of all outcome values in the model is made in a hierarchical sequence by processing if-then statements that set the outcome variable value for all semesters in the study. Table 2.1 illustrates the outcomes for the same student for each of five semesters. Boldface depicts a change in status for the student from one step in the process classification process to the next.

Step 2A: Distinguish Persisters and Unknowns. A persister is a student who continues to be enrolled at the college; an unknown is a student whose student ID is not found in the Semester Course file. To determine which students are persisters or unknowns, process each Semester Course file in chronological sequence using SAS or a similar analysis tool. A variable named for the semester (for example, SP05) is created. If the student ID is found in the cohort file and in the spring 2005 Semester Course file, the value for variable SP05 is coded as persist. If the student ID is found in the cohort file but not in the SP05 Semester Course file, the value for variable SP05 is coded as unknown. The same is done for the fall 2005 semester (FA05) file. A variable named FA05 is created and assigned a value of persist or unknown depending on whether the student ID matches between

Table 2.1. Student Outcomes by Semester

Step	Description of Step	Student ID	SP05	FA05	SP06	FA06	SP07
2a	Distinguish persisters and unknowns	111111	Persist	Unknown	Unknown	Persist	Unknown
2b	Determine stop outs	111111	Persist	**StopOut**	**StopOut**	Persist	Unknown
2c	Determine transfers	111111	Persist	StopOut	StopOut	Persist	**Transfer**
2d	Determine certificate completers	111111	Persist	StopOut	StopOut	**Cert**	Transfer
2e	Determine degree completers	111111	Persist	StopOut	StopOut	**Degree**	Transfer

the cohort file and the FA05 Semester Course file. This is done for every semester in the study. The variables FA04 (from which the cohort is defined in this example), SP05, FA05, SP06, FA06, and SP07 are created for each student in the cohort. Each variable has a value of either persist or unknown.

The results shown in Table 2.1 resemble a slot machine. This is a good analogy because it is easy to imagine a slot machine with a wheel for each semester. The possible student outcomes used by the tracking model are placed in sequence on each wheel. The values of each wheel click into place as the sequence steps are processed. Table 2.1 indicates that a student in the cohort with student ID 111111 was enrolled or persisted in SP05 and FA06 but was not enrolled or unknown in FA05, SP06, and SP07.

Step 2B: Determine Stop Outs. Step 2B determines if an unknown is really a stop out, a student who was not enrolled in the semester under study but did reenroll in a future semester. Logical if-then statements are again used to establish this value for each student in the cohort. Looking at Table 2.1, we see that the value for variable FA06 is persist. So although student 111111 did not persist in either FA05 or SP06, the values for the variables need to be changed from unknown to stop out. The logic is this: if FA06 equals persist and FA05 equals unknown, then FA05 equals stop out, and if FA06 equals persist and SP06 equals unknown, then SP06 equals stop out. Although the coding may seem tedious, it can be done very quickly and efficiently by copying and using search and replace. The coding logic used to create the other outcome values is very similar. Table 2.1 shows the changes to the slot machine resulting from this recoding.

At this point, it is useful to mention that the order in which changes are made in the slot machine matters because some outcomes are considered more important than others. For example, this model was developed to generate information to be used to complete the community college IPEDS GRS survey. In this model, degrees are more valued than certificates or transfers. So the last values that will be determined for the semester variable will be about degree and certificate completion. This presents another issue with the model. It is possible, and even likely, that some students in the cohort will have multiple outcomes or values for a semester. Obviously, it would not be unusual for a student to both persist and graduate during the same semester. It is a limitation of the model that forces the researcher to decide the order or sequence in which variable values are established. The most important ones are established last.

Step 2C: Determine Transfers. Step 2B determines if any students in the cohort transferred to another postsecondary institution. External data about student enrollments at other postsecondary institutions are needed to make these determinations. One's ability to obtain these data depends on many factors. The first concern is legal considerations related to FERPA that may limit an IR office's ability to obtain transfer data. FERPA does not have to be a major obstacle if care is taken to make the appropriate data-sharing agreements. A typical source for these data is a direct agreement with other postsecondary institutions, state higher education files, or the National Student Clearinghouse. This model assumes that external unit record transfer data with student IDs are available by semester. It is necessary to create a Master Transfer file using the same methodology used to create the Master Degree file.

Step 2C is to determine if the values of unknown or persist should be recoded and changed to transfer. A transfer is a student who is known to be enrolled at a different institution during a semester. This model relies on the premise that a transfer is more successful than a persister or a student whose status is unknown. Logical if-then statements are used to establish this value for each student in the cohort. Looking at Table 2.1, we find the value for variable SP07 is unknown. However, there was a match in the Transfer File for student 111111 for the variable SP07. So, the value of variable SP07 is changed from unknown to transfer. The logic is this: if SP07 equals unknown or SP07 equals persist or SP07 equals stop out and in the Master Transfer file SP07 equals transfer, then SP07 in the slot machine equals transfer. The value of SP07 is changed from unknown to transfer for student 111111. Table 2.2 shows the change to the slot machine.

Step 2D: Determine Certificate Completers. Step 2D determines if any of the students in the cohort graduated with either a certificate or an associate degree. If student 111111 earned a certificate in any of the semesters covered by the study, the value for each semester variable is changed from persist, stop out, transfer, or unknown to certificate (coded as cert). So variable FA06 in the slot machine is changed from persist to certificate.

Step 2E: Determine Degree Completers. Step 2E follows the same process as used to determine certificate completers. Because student 111111 earned both a certificate and a degree in the FA06 semester, the value of variable

Table 2.2. Persistence and Completion

Cohort: First-Time Full-Time Degree-Seeking Students; N = 250	SP07	
	Frequency	Percent
Persist	60	24.0
Stop out	0	0
Transfer	5	2.0
Certificate	15	6.0
Degree	20	8.0
Unknown	150	60.0
Total	250	100.0

FA06 is changed from cert to degree. This is done because the researcher has used a trumping rule that considers earning a degree to be more important than earning a certificate. Here is the final logic: if FA06 equals unknown or FA06 equals persist or FA06 equals stop out or FA06 equals transfer or FA06 equals cert and in the Master Degree file FA06 equals degree, then FA06 equals degree. The value of FA06 is changed because FA06 equaled certificate for student 111111. Table 2.3 shows the change to the slot machine.

Step Three: Analyze the Data. The basic pieces of the student tracking model are in place. For each student in the cohort, we know the student's behavior in each semester: persistence, stop out, transfer, earned a certificate, earned a degree, or unknown. The researcher next must analyze the results for the model. This is done by counting the number of students with each value in each of the semester variables SP05, FA05, SP06, FA06, and SP07. Variable SP07 is especially important because it shows the final frequency count for each value (persist, stop out, transfer, certificate, degree, and unknown). The total frequency count for the values of the cohort for each semester (variable) must be equal to the total count in the study cohort.

Table 2.2 gives an example of this frequency distribution. The researcher will notice problems with this analysis. First, the frequency count for the stop out value is 0. This is because of the logic used to create the value. It is known that these students returned because we have the student's enrollment information for subsequent semesters. There is no subsequent semester to SP07 in this model because it is the last year for which we have semester data files. The final semester in the study will always show a stop out count of 0. These students are best understood by looking at earlier semesters in the study.

Another problem is that the model does not fully report the swirl effects of students who may transfer and return, earn a certificate and a degree, or earn a degree and then return to college to take more classes. The model deals with these conditions by creating additional values. The complexity of the logical if-then statements increases as more outcome variable values are added to the model. These values are sequenced in the order in which

Table 2.3. Persistence and Completion by Semester

	FA04		SP05		FA05		SP06		FA06		SP07	
Degree			0	0%	0	0%	7	3%	7	3%	20	8%
Certificate			0	0%	3	1%	2	1%	0	0%	15	6%
Persisted	250	100%	166	66%	115	46%	94	38%	77	31%	60	24%
Stop out			28	11%	30	12%	17	7%	10	4%	0	0%
Transfer			1	0%	7	3%	1	0%	10	4%	5	2%
Unknown			55	22%	95	38%	126	50%	140	56%	150	60%
Not enrolled, completed degree			0	0%	0	0%	0	0%	5	2%	0	0%
Not enrolled, completed certificate			0	0%	0	0%	1	0%	0	0%	0	0%
Enrolled after completion			0	0%	0	0%	2	1%	0	0%	0	0%
Earned degree after certificate			0	0%	0	0%	0	0%	1	0%	0	0%
Earned additional certificate			0	0%	0	0%	0	0%	0	0%	0	0%
Earned additional degree			0	0%	0	0%	0	0%	0	0%	0	0%
Total students in cohort	250		250		250		250		250		250	
Cumulative degrees			0	0%	0	0%	7	3%	14	6%	34	14%
Cumulative certificates			0	0%	3	1%	5	2%	5	2%	20	8%
Total unique completers			0	0%	3	1%	12	5%	19	8%	54	22%

Summary for model	FA04	SP05	FA05	SP06	FA06	SP07
Completer		0%	1%	5%	8%	22%
Persisted	100%	66%	46%	38%	31%	24%
Stop out		11%	12%	7%	4%	0%
Transfer		0%	3%	0%	4%	2%
Unknown		22%	38%	50%	56%	60%

they appear in the model. The value FinDeg is processed first. I have given an illustration of how the value is shown in Table 2.3, which summarizes model results for the FA04 cohort.

Value FinDeg counts the number of students who completed or finished a degree and did not enroll again; it appears in the table as *not enrolled, completed degree*. Value FinCert counts the number of students who completed or finished a certificate and did not enroll again; it appears in the table as *not enrolled, completed certificate*. Value Back counts the number of students who came back to college after completing a certificate or degree; it appears in the table as back. Value 1st Deg counts the number of students who are awarded their first degree after they were awarded a certificate; it appears in the table as *earned degree after certificate*. Value X Cert counts the number of students who earned a second certificate; it appears in the table as *earned additional certificate*. Value X Deg counts the number of students who earned a second degree; it appears in the table as *earned additional degree*.

There is another, larger problem with the SP07 frequency distribution in Table 2.3 that the researcher must solve. The table shows the number of certificates and degrees as fifteen and twenty. However, these are just the counts for SP07 and do not include students who may have earned a degree or certificate in an earlier semester, or students who were awarded more than one certificate or degree during the semesters in the study. One easy way to solve this problem is to use a spreadsheet to analyze the data and calculate a cumulative count of completers in the study cohort. This process could be automated using SAS or SPSS; transferring the model results from SAS or SPSS output to a spreadsheet takes little time and gives the researcher an opportunity to better understand the numbers and interpret the results.

Step Four: Use a Spreadsheet to Calculate Total Completers. Start by creating a new value called completer. A completer is a student who earns a certificate or degree. Begin by determining when the student was awarded a certificate and then determine when the student was awarded a degree. The goal is to find the total number of students who first completed for each semester by summing the count for first degree or first certificate. By developing a completer value that accumulates the number of first certificates and degrees, it is possible to show the model's most important completion outcomes results.

Step Five: Show the Results. In addition to presenting results in tables, stacked column charts are especially useful to illustrate the results for subsets of the cohort. Results can be put into a spreadsheet to produce charts or transferred to PowerPoint. In that application, toggling between charts can emphasize differences between subgroups. Figures 2.1 and 2.2 show model results for students new to the college in fall 2004 who did and did not pass developmental English. The differences are immediately evident; note especially the increased percentage of persisters for members of the cohort who passed developmental English compared to those who did not, and the corresponding reduction in the percentage of students in the "unknown" category.

Figure 2.1. New Students, Fall 2004, Passed Developmental English

	FA 04	SP 05	FA 05	SP 06	FA 06	SP 07
Unknown		7%	23%	39%	49%	60%
Stop out		4%	7%	6%	4%	0%
Persisted	100%	89%	70%	56%	47%	39%
Completer		0%	0%	0%	0%	1%

Note: N taking course = 1,140; N passing course = 900.

The Student Tracking Model Can Evolve

The student tracking model can become very complex if the researcher has available historical data and adds additional values to the model. Such a model may be needed to adequately explain quite complex student behavior. For example, researchers may find it useful to refine the transfer data to

Figure 2.2. New Students, Fall 2004, Did Not Pass Developmental English

	FA 04	SP 05	FA 05	SP 06	FA 06	SP 07
Unknown		67%	75%	81%	88%	100%
Stop out		0%	8%	6%	3%	0%
Persisted	100%	33%	17%	13%	9%	0%
Completer		0%	0%	0%	0%	0%

Note: N taking course = 1,140; N not passing course = 240.

NEW DIRECTIONS FOR COMMUNITY COLLEGES • DOI: 10.1002/cc

identify the institutions to which a large number of students transfer and to depict students who earn a degree after transfer. Other values that might be added to the model are the number of times a student transfers to another college and whether the student returns to the home college after transferring. The research could also examine majors and degrees earned at transfer institutions, if data are available.

A Student Tracking Model is a useful tool for institutional offices. It allows the researcher to select a student cohort to study on the basis of student attributes or performance. The cohort can be tracked over time and outcomes charted to produce a picture of student success. It takes time to create a Student Tracking Model, but the results it produces will be well worth the effort.

FRED LILLIBRIDGE *is the campus institutional effectiveness and planning officer at Doña Ana Community College in Las Cruces, New Mexico.*

NEW DIRECTIONS FOR COMMUNITY COLLEGES • DOI: 10.1002/cc

3

This chapter describes several examples of institutional use of state- and college-level tracking data to benchmark performance, improve student success, and enhance program effectiveness.

Using Student Tracking Data from an Institutional Perspective

Joanne Bashford

Florida adopted a set of comprehensive accountability measures for community colleges in the 1990s. They included tracking student cohorts to determine student enrollment from high school to college, successful completion of college preparatory (remedial) courses within a two-year period, retention and graduation rates after three years, job placement rate after graduation, and transfer student performance in the state university system. Miami Dade College (MDC) uses these measures to identify areas where institutional performance is lower than for the community college system as a whole or a subset of peer colleges.

Many of these measures subsequently became part of the MDC Core Indicators Report for institutional effectiveness. This report uses color-coded, directional arrows to reflect trends in MDC's performance relative to state community college and national benchmarks. Indicators were chosen to generate meaningful information related to the college's mission, vision, and strategic goals. MDC's executive committee reviews the Core Indicator Report each year and can easily see areas that need improvement. The committee then offers direction and resources to the appropriate units within the college to design and implement strategies to improve performance.

In addition to the accountability measure reports, the Florida Department of Education produces ad hoc longitudinal reports on student outcomes. MDC uses these reports to validate its local research and benchmark performance against peer colleges in Florida. Two recent state reports calculated the five-year success rate for first-time student cohorts to examine the efficacy of Student Life Skills (SLS) courses and the impact of varying levels of remedial need.

NEW DIRECTIONS FOR COMMUNITY COLLEGES, no. 143, Fall 2008 © 2008 Wiley Periodicals, Inc.
Published online in Wiley InterScience (www.interscience.wiley.com) • DOI: 10.1002/cc.333

This chapter presents several examples of how MDC uses state data to benchmark local performance and work toward improvement. The first example, success in mathematics, describes extensive local research leading to program change. The next example, college preparatory success, underscores the need to continue support for underprepared students. The usefulness of an SLS course was already established at MDC, but in the next example state data led to efforts to improve the content of these courses. Finally, the chapter concludes with an example focused on improving the graduation rate.

Improving Student Success in Mathematics

Early accountability data on student completion of remedial courses indicated that the completion rate for mathematics was lower than for reading or writing, and lower than the statewide average. The two-year completion rate for college preparatory mathematics was slightly over 40 percent in the early 1990s, while the rates for reading and writing preparatory coursework were as high as 60 percent. As a result, local studies were conducted on student progress through both remedial and college-level mathematics. It was clear that mathematics was a significant barrier to student progression and success, with notable attrition points throughout the math course sequence. MDC identified specific remedial and college-level mathematics courses as high-risk for students through analysis of courses with high enrollment and the lowest success rate. Pass and withdrawal rates were examined in this analysis in an attempt to identify some of the reasons students experienced difficulty in the courses.

MDC conducted several analyses to determine if the low success rate in specific math courses was due to inaccurate placement or inadequate preparation related to prerequisite course competencies. Placement test scores and subsequent student course grades were evaluated to identify the ranges that yielded the best estimate of students' readiness for specific courses. Progression analyses reviewed the pass rate for students who enrolled in the next course in the math sequence immediately following successful completion of the prerequisite course and compared their performance with students who tested directly into the course. This analysis revealed that prerequisite courses were not affording adequate preparation for the subsequent courses because students who were placed directly into the courses were more successful. In addition, the institutional research office analyzed the pass rate for students who delayed taking the next mathematics course in the sequence (as many students tend to do). Not surprisingly, students who were continuously enrolled in the courses were more successful than students who took a break between mathematics course enrollments. Mathematics faculty reviewed these data to identify opportunities to improve alignment in course competencies, develop strategies to discourage students from stopping out of the math course sequence, and encourage students to begin taking mathematics courses earlier.

NEW DIRECTIONS FOR COMMUNITY COLLEGES • DOI: 10.1002/cc

The college also conducted focus groups to hear students' perspectives about the difficulties they experienced in high-risk mathematics courses. Students identified instructional strategies and approaches that helped them learn the material, such as guided practice and opportunities to work on mathematics problems during class time. They also acknowledged that attending class regularly, keeping up with assignments, asking questions in class, receiving frequent feedback on performance, and using computer and study skills labs were critical.

The institutional research office presented and discussed these data with faculty in a series of math roundtables, which led to development of a variety of innovative ideas to enhance student success. In addition to curricular revisions, strategies championed by faculty included learning communities, mandatory study sessions, nontraditional teaching methods such as project-based and collaborative instruction, labs with special math tutoring software, and math anxiety workshops. As these strategies were implemented, the institutional research office compiled data on their efficacy. The current accountability data show a completion rate of 58 percent for college preparatory mathematics, a substantial increase over the 1993 completion rate of 40 percent, suggesting that these targeted efforts have made a real difference in student success.

Given the success of using data to improve student performance in the mathematics courses, faculty in other disciplines have established focused research agendas in partnership with institutional research to examine student progression. Finally, as part of the college's reaccreditation, MDC proposed a Quality Enhancement Plan (QEP) focused on mathematics. Both the state accountability data and the information collected in the mathematics-focused research are serving as benchmarks for the success of the QEP.

Examining Five-Year Success Rates by Initial Placement Status and Ethnicity

As part of the project, the institutional research office used the state longitudinal study to examine five-year outcomes for cohorts of first-time-in-college (FTIC) students who began in the fall of 2001. The academic success measure (graduated, still enrolled, or transferred) was used. Additionally, employment status was added to this measure to create an additional overall successful outcome measure. Students were again divided on the basis of type and number of remedial courses needed and their ethnicity.

A look at the cohorts showed that MDC's college-ready students (non-remedial) had a higher graduation rate (43 percent) than at any of its six peer colleges in Florida. However, MDC had a higher proportion of students who needed remediation (80 percent, versus 76 percent systemwide) and who needed remediation in all three basic skills areas (32 percent, versus 25 percent systemwide). These system- and institutional-level data also revealed that the graduation rate was lowest for students who needed remediation in all three areas. This finding is important; other longitudinal data do not consider student course-taking patterns when comparing graduation rates among colleges, even though it is reasonable to expect students who need more remediation will have a lower graduation rate.

Consistent with MDC's own internal research, this state study indicated that students who needed remediation in mathematics alone or in combination with other subject areas had a lower success rate than students who were college-ready in mathematics. This reinforced MDC's emphasis on mathematics and the need for innovative strategies to enhance student success, such as the examples that were discussed earlier.

Outcomes by ethnicity revealed that Hispanic students had the highest academic success rate of ethnic groups, at MDC and systemwide. African American students were most likely to need remediation (90 percent at MDC and 80 percent systemwide) and had the lowest academic success rate at MDC. Although MDC's rate compared favorably with the system as a whole, the data underscored the need for resources, support, supplemental instruction, and a culture of engagement to help underprepared students meet the challenges of higher education.

Examining the Impact of Student Life Skills Courses

One important way in which Miami Dade College offers additional support and college connection to underprepared students is through the Student Life Skills courses. These courses cover study skills, note taking, time management, test-taking strategies, and career exploration in an interactive and supportive environment. MDC conducted a study in the late 1990s and found that underprepared students who co-enrolled in a college preparatory course and an SLS course had a higher course pass rate and higher fall-to-spring retention rate than their peers who did not take an SLS course. On the basis of these findings, the college required students who were enrolling in college preparatory courses to take an SLS course concurrently. In 2005, however, it became apparent that many students were bypassing the requirement because of unintended consequences of registration system changes. Because of this, Institutional Research was able to identify a comparison group of students who did not take the required SLS course and thereby repeat the study to determine if the same positive outcomes would be evident for students who took the SLS course. This second study obtained similar results: students who took the SLS course concurrently with college preparatory courses had a higher course pass rate and better retention rate.

The state longitudinal studies encompassed a longer timeframe and examined five-year outcomes for FTIC students who began in the fall of 1999. Measures included graduation and a broader measure of academic success (graduated, still enrolled, or transferred). Student results were disaggregated by the type and number of remedial courses needed and by whether or not they took an SLS course. The academic success rate of MDC students who took the course was more than ten percentage points higher than for students who did not take the course. Students who needed remediation in all three basic skills areas had a success rate that was twenty-one percentage points higher if they also took the SLS course, and the rate was twenty-four percentage points higher for students who needed remediation in both math and writing.

Though these findings were positive, student success gains from the SLS course at MDC were not as large for some student groups as those statewide. Additionally, the state study showed a positive impact for colleges that required the SLS course for students who are academically prepared for college-level courses (college-ready). From these findings, MDC is exploring course competencies at high-performing community colleges and examining how to enhance the SLS course. For example, MDC may link the SLS courses with college preparatory content area courses to furnish practical applications of skills learned in the SLS course and reinforce learning overall. Another advantage of this approach is that it fosters connections and engagement between students as a community of learners in the paired courses. MDC may also consider recommending the SLS course for college-ready students as a part of the first-year experience programs.

Increasing Completion Rate in the Associate in Science Programs

Accountability data on the graduation rate for associate in science students indicated that MDC's rate was lower than the statewide average, but the success rate of students is high (almost 90 percent). The state accountability success rate includes students who graduated, who were still enrolled in good standing, or who left in good standing. The data showed that a high proportion of associate in science students were leaving in good standing, suggesting they had achieved at least an intermediate educational goal.

MDC's Office of Institutional Research presented detailed student data to program managers showing program enrollments and completions. Transcript analysis of students in some program areas such as business and technology clearly indicated that students were acquiring work skills and then leaving the college before completing a degree. Two strategies were adopted to better measure student accomplishments: establishment of shorter credit certificates and creation of a Web-based program review system.

The college established shorter credit certificates as part of the full associate in science degree in programs where component competencies were sufficient for job entry. Students could earn a certificate as they progressed, and the completion would be recorded in the official college data. If students left for employment before graduating, the college would have a record of their earning the shorter certificate(s) for immediate job entry. However, additional research showed that many students did not declare these shorter certificates as their goal; instead, they declared the full associate in science program. Within the past year, a new system has been developed for "degree shopping." The matrix of courses for each credit certificate was programmed and compared with the coursework taken by associate in science degree-seeking students. If coursework indicated that the student had earned a certificate en route to the degree, the certificate was awarded and the student received a congratulatory letter. Using this method, many of the students who leave before completing an associate in science degree earn a certificate acknowledging courses taken, and students who are still enrolled receive encouragement to continue.

The second strategy to monitor the progress of associate in science students was creation of a Web-based program review system. This system included several unique features to highlight student progress and program effectiveness: the number of students who reach certain program completion benchmarks, the number in key courses usually taken toward the end of the program, the number of graduates, the number placed in jobs related to their degree or certificate, and labor market data related to the program. Managers can see the number of students who completed 25 percent, 50 percent, and 75 percent of the program coursework (program benchmarks) and the students who are leaving after completing only part of a specific program. This supplies helpful information for establishing shorter certificates.

Comparing the number of students in key courses with the number who declared the program intent encourages faculty to counsel students on their career choice and update records for accuracy in program intent. In addition, comparing the number of students in the key courses with the actual number of graduates highlights programs where students leave just short of the degree. Faculty teaching these courses can now emphasize the benefits of completing a degree. Finally, placement rate (generated by state-level tracking) and labor market data present important information about demand and earning potential for graduates of the programs.

Summary

These examples illustrate a few of the many institutional opportunities to make effective use of state- and college-level student tracking data. By tracking cohorts, colleges are able to identify barriers to student progression. By benchmarking cohort performance, colleges are able to identify promising strategies to improve student success. A key lesson that emerges from these examples is that global state data can alert institutional researchers and complement institutional data in examining practical opportunities to improve student success. These same state data can serve as useful benchmarks to evaluate the effectiveness of new strategies as they are implemented.

JOANNE BASHFORD *is the associate provost for institutional effectiveness at Miami Dade College.*

NEW DIRECTIONS FOR COMMUNITY COLLEGES • DOI: 10.1002/cc

4

This chapter describes the evolution, content, and use of Florida's unit record system, which includes data on K–20 students and staff. It presents examples of how information derived from tracking is used both for state-level policy making and institution-level research and practice.

A Statewide Student Unit Record System: Florida as a Case Study

Jay Pfeiffer, Patricia Windham

Like Trudy Bers, Jay wrote about student tracking systems for an issue of *New Directions for Community Colleges* about twenty years ago. In it, Jay described Florida's automated follow-up system, called the Florida Education and Training Placement Information Program, affectionately known as FETPIP. Since then, the FETPIP system has continued to mature, was authorized in state law, and became a national model of how administrative data can be used to develop reliable, objective, and detailed information about what happens to students after they leave a community college or a particular program.

The FETPIP is an interagency data collection system that obtains follow-up data on former students. It is the nation's longest continuous operation of its type, originally established by the Florida legislature in 1984 and codified in state law in 1987. In this chapter, we describe how this student tracking approach has grown into an integrated, longitudinal education system in Florida that permits compiling data about students across all parts of the Florida education system and offers information about their participation in the Florida labor market.

The View from the State

This is a topic of great interest because the U.S. Department of Education has been aggressively funding and directing creation of state-level, longitudinal data systems that link K–12 and postsecondary education. Although

the FETPIP was historically an organizational offshoot of the Florida Department of Education's primary student and staff data systems, it is now an integral part of those systems.

Organization. The Florida Department of Education has taken an organizational approach that locates its major student and staff databases in one division. Referred to as the Division of Accountability, Research, and Measurement, it is responsible not only for operating and maintaining these databases but also for maintaining key data exchange relationships with other state agencies, notably the Florida Board of Governors, Independent Colleges and Universities of Florida, Department of Children and Families, the Agency for Workforce Innovation, the Department of Juvenile Justice, and the Department of Corrections. It also maintains data exchange relationships with national data source organizations such as the National Student Clearinghouse, the College Board, ACT, the Federal Employment Data Exchange System, and the Wage Record Interchange System. Consolidating these functions facilitates coordination on a variety of data collection and access issues, among them collection cycles and methods, data element definitions, security, exchange protocols, access, research, and reporting.

Source Systems. The key databases in the division include what can be referred to as source systems. These systems are student and staff data collection processes that are regularly reported to the state department by school districts and community colleges on the basis of reporting protocols and definitions promulgated by the department. The division also coordinates all elements of the state's assessment programs. These programs include the Florida Comprehensive Assessment Tests in reading, math, science, and writing, which are administered each year to K–12 students; the College Placement Test; the rising junior program for students moving upward in higher education; and some forty-two subject area examinations for K–12 educators. The student and staff database for the state university system is another important source system that is periodically accessed. The division also maintains integrated, longitudinal education data systems; there is one single database that includes K–20 data for all students across all years and connects these data to other data resources such as employment, financial aid, and welfare participation.

Student and Staff Source Systems. Florida's public education system is recognized for the breadth of the data resources maintained by the Department of Education. In cooperation with public school districts, technical centers, community colleges, and universities, information is collected that describes the educational progress of students along with related program and administrative information. Data are used to meet federal and state statutory requirements for reporting and accountability. They are used to monitor and manage educational programs in classrooms, and for managers at the local and state levels. The data are also fundamental to information exchanges such as transcripts between students and educational institutions. The systems include:

- Student information systems for public schools, adult and career and technical centers, community colleges, and universities
- Finance and accounting information systems for each delivery sector
- Student assessment databases
- Student financial aid data for postsecondary education
- Student financial aid data for K–12 scholarships
- Facilities information for each delivery sector

These data largely deal with enrollment characteristics and academic progress of students as they move through the public school system, into postsecondary institutions, and to the labor force. The data originate with local school districts, community colleges, and universities. They are compiled from student registration information, classroom performance information, and local finance and accounting systems.

Each information system includes data dictionaries, comprehensive sets of data elements, edits, transmission management reports, and other tools that furnish consistent and accurate data to the state department. Once collected, data are housed on multiple database platforms including DB2, Oracle, SQL Server, Sun Solaris, and Windows operating systems. Various reports are generated from these databases to meet local, state, and federal reporting needs. These reports are made available in various forms, among them hard copy and electronic delivery mechanisms.

Applications. The term *applications* refers to the programs and organizations that receive follow-up data collection services. Currently there are more than 120 applications. These applications are used to analyze all public school system high school graduates and dropouts, all community college associate degree and vocational students, all secondary and postsecondary vocational students, all state university system graduates, adult education and GED students, selected private vocational schools students, welfare reform participants, unemployment insurance claimants, and all correctional system releases. Smaller operations such as adult migrant education, blind services, apprenticeship, certain longitudinal collections, and others are included as well.

Organizations representing each application give FETPIP individual student or participant files from their management information system units. The files include individual identifiers as well as demographic, socioeconomic, and programmatic data. In the most recent data collection cycle, these applications yielded FETPIP nearly eighteen million program-level records representing about eight million individuals.

Data Collection. FETPIP collects follow-up data that describe the employment, military enlistment, incarceration, public assistance participation, and continuing education experience of the participants being followed. It accomplishes data collection by electronically linking participant files to the administrative records of other state and federal agencies. It also links to Florida's K–20 Education Data Warehouse (EDW). The warehouse was created to integrate data from twenty-six state-level operational source systems and afford a view across systems reflecting the K–20 public education environment. Data from the existing source systems are loaded into the EDW on the basis of a common set of business rules and definitions. Because the records are already matched in the EDW and the large stores of data are in one database, it is possible for data products to be generated quickly. The EDW is historical in nature, and new terms and years of data are added as they become available. In addition, the EDW includes new sources of data that enhance the K–20 education picture.

Data. The initial development and population of the EDW was conducted primarily through a vendor contract from January 2001 through May 2003. As a result of that development, these are the data currently in the EDW:

- Student demographic, enrollment, educational programs, promotion, attendance, and test score trends
- Educational institution information
- Financial aid records
- Student employment history
- Course offerings
- Educational staff information
- Educational awards
- Educational facilities information
- Financial information

Personally identifiable data are not stored in the data warehouse. During the matching process, a randomly generated unique identification number is assigned; personally identifiable data such as the source student identification number, name, and birth date are not loaded. Currently, only EDW staff can access the warehouse database. Any request for data at the detail level must go through a high-level approval process before release of data.

Example Applications

A partial list of example applications that cut across time, educational sectors, and the workforce are provided here with brief annotations. Together they illustrate the range and diversity of issues that can be explored and studies that can be conducted using a data system like Florida's.

Workforce Estimating. Twice each year, a Workforce Estimating Conference is convened to present official information to the Florida legislature regarding the demand for certain kinds of jobs in Florida's economy as well as production of trained and educated workers for those jobs. This is a unique marriage of labor statistics with enrollment, completion, and placement data from the integrated education data systems. The data are used to target certain vocational and academic disciplines for special funding, financial aid, or other attention.

NEW DIRECTIONS FOR COMMUNITY COLLEGES • DOI: 10.1002/cc

Follow-up Information. The FETPIP program has long supplied information through reports and special analyses that explore statistics about what happens with students after they leave education at every level. The term leave education means that a student has left with or without an education credential. These reports include employment and earnings, military enlistments, continuing postsecondary or adult education, public assistance participation, and incarceration. The data can be very detailed with respect to the characteristics of students as well as employment and other follow-up factors. The data have also been collected and displayed longitudinally for examination of the period from just after leaving a program to several years later.

Costs of Dropping Out. The department engaged in a targeted study of costs associated with dropping out of school. This analysis combined data from the EDW regarding students who dropped out of high school, employment and unemployment data from FETPIP, public assistance data from the Department of Children and Families, data from adult general education and GED programs, data from the Agency for Workforce Innovation regarding workforce Investment Act programs, and data from vocational and community college resources. The purpose was to ascertain the social costs of dropping out and compare them to costs associated with successful interventions. Social costs come in the form of unemployment, public assistance, adult education, and incarceration relative to earnings for dropouts in comparison to students with a higher level of educational attainment. The study found there is a substantial savings when students complete high school with a standard diploma.

Postsecondary Access. There have been at least four efforts to examine issues related to the accessibility of postsecondary education. In Florida, this meant three task forces initiated by the state board of education and the university system's board of governors.

Higher Education Funding Advisory Committee. In 2002, the board of education formed a Higher Education Funding Advisory Committee. Although the committee focused more on funding and financial aid, it also addressed a number of issues related to student transitions from K–12 into postsecondary education and retention of students between their freshman and sophomore years. As part of the process, the staff developed a student flow model that allowed policy makers to test a theoretical intervention and see projected results based on current Florida K–20 pipelines. The committee's work constituted the foundation for the board's legislative agenda in 2003.

Postsecondary Education Access Task Force. In 2005, the chairs of the boards of education and governors formed a Postsecondary Education Access Task Force (ATF) to follow up on the work of the previous task force. The ATF focused on the demand for higher education from both student and labor market perspectives. On the student side, the department used the EDW to project the number of high school graduates, the number of high school graduates entering postsecondary education, as well as students entering postsecondary education who were not recent graduates to

NEW DIRECTIONS FOR COMMUNITY COLLEGES • DOI: 10.1002/cc

illustrate growing demand brought about by a combination of student population growth, school reform, and labor market demands.

Go Higher, Florida! Task Force. As a part of a grant from the National Governor's Association, the State Board of Education formed the Go Higher, Florida! task force. Data presentations from the EDW included analysis of the changing demographics of students moving from elementary through middle and into high school in comparison to the characteristics of students at various postsecondary sectors. The analyses included a great deal of longitudinal information on education credentials, employment, and earnings.

Commission on the Future of Higher Education. In 2006, the secretary of the U.S. Department of Education formed the Commission on the Future of Higher Education, popularly known as the Spellings Commission. One of the commission's featured interests related to higher education accountability and establishment of a national student-level database (referred to as a national unit record system). Florida's experiences were discussed in some detail at a commission hearing held in Indianapolis in 2006.

High School Feedback. Through the EDW, the department offers an annual online feedback report to all Florida high schools that gives basic information about their students' preparation and initial success in postsecondary education. This includes SAT, ACT, and College Placement Test results, as well as information regarding student entrance into postsecondary education. Longitudinal data as to ultimate success of students in postsecondary education are available as well.

K–20 Accountability. The Florida legislature enacted a law referred to as the K20 accountability program in 2002. It required that the state board of education develop a system of accountability measures that addressed four educational goals. Fulfillment of these measures is subject to a performance funding process of up to 10 percent of the annual legislative appropriations for each education sector. The basic idea is that each sector—K–12, workforce education, adult education, community colleges, and universities—would have a set of metrics that address each goal in a similar fashion.

The Teacher Pipeline. The Florida legislature asked the department of education to develop a process that would assist policy makers in identifying educator preparation processes that are particularly successful in placing teacher preparation graduates into Florida classrooms. To do this, researchers used longitudinal data in the EDW to focus on preparation programs in public universities and track the progress of students from their initial entrance into the university or a community college, through their progress into the upper division, and into Florida classrooms (or other employment venues). The data flow has included information about retention in the classroom as well as attachment of employed graduates to the students they teach. The objective is to identify key measures that can be used to make note of program initiatives that are particularly successful in training teachers, placing and retaining them in the classroom, and helping them succeed with respect to student learning.

These are examples of some of the work that has been supported by Florida's integrated, longitudinal education data systems. It is not an exhaustive list but suggests some important subject areas that can be addressed when the notion of longitudinal education data systems includes linkages between K–12 systems, adult systems, and community colleges and other higher education systems. These linkages should be seen as mutually beneficial. They can inform policy for all sectors and be used to identify points between the systems where significant improvements need to be made.

The View from the State Community College Agency

One of the challenging aspects of using data contained in a centrally located database is to turn the various data elements into a cohesive piece of information. The Florida Division of Community Colleges determined that the millions of dollars spent in developing and implementing the community college Student Data Base (SDB) afforded a rare opportunity to use the data elements for research into numerous areas of student access, retention, and success, where success includes attainment of awards such as certification and degrees, transferring to four-year institutions, and completing personal educational goals.

The division set aside one full-time-equivalent (FTE) position to concentrate on using the SDB to compare the Florida Community College System (FCCS) trends against national trends and those in other states. The incumbent was given full access to the SDB and directed to explore issues as they arose. The full access allowed the person to work in an exploratory manner without the need to involve other programmers. Because the files are stored on an internal server located within the Florida Department of Education, there was no need to be concerned about the cost of multiple runs resulting from numerous what-if scenarios or programming errors.

This freedom has led to multiple longitudinal studies that often combine five or six years of data. The most common cohort studied is an incoming set of students identified as being first-time-in-college (FTIC) who are tracked via their reported student identifier across time. This ability to combine types of data across years allows the division to determine outcomes for these students. Because the State University System's Student Data Course File (SDCF) is also shared with the division, it is possible to determine if an FCCS student transferred to the State University System (SUS).

Florida also has contracts with the National Student Clearinghouse to track students who transfer outside our state public institutions, and with the state's Agency for Workforce Innovation to track students into the labor market. All of these resources mean that the state is able to supply information on who earns awards, who transfers, and who is employed.

Comparisons Across Institutions. The division has produced two main types of longitudinal analysis. The first is a comparison of incoming cohorts. Fall 1993, 1997, 1999, and 2001 FTIC students were tracked for five years to determine their graduation, transfer, and still-enrolled rates. These groups were also disaggregated into the major ethnic and racial race groups in Florida. The results are shared with each institution in the FCCS. Using these files, the institutions can compare their results with those of their peers and the state as a whole. They can also determine potential achievement gaps for groups of students and find institutions that might have better results.

Cohort Analyses. The second major way to use longitudinal data is to analyze a specific cohort subgroup on the basis of an additional characteristic or course-taking pattern. For example, a cohort may be divided into students who received Pell grants and those who did not. The same outcomes can then be determined for each group and the results compared.

A recent study of this type investigated the impact that taking an SLS course has on a cohort. The study not only considered whether a student took the course but also disaggregated the cohort according to whether students had started their academic career as full-time or part-time, their ethnicity, and their entering need for different levels of developmental education.

The results of this study indicated that an SLS course was beneficial to students no matter their characteristics. This information has been shared with the FCCS and caused several institutions to require that entering students enroll in the course. By having a centralized database, it is possible to determine the potential impact this change has on practice.

By using both the SDB and SDCF, the state can track graduates of a given program from one institution to another, or to another part of the higher education system. For example, nursing graduates who complete the associate's degree at a community college are tracked to determine whether they transfer to a university to earn a bachelor's degree in order to move into administration or prepare themselves for other options.

Tracking from one system to another allows more detailed analyses of who transfers and who does not. Work done in this area several years ago indicated that the factors of gender and ethnicity or race paled in comparison to age when considering who went from the FCCS to the SUS. It was also possible to determine if proximity to an institution was involved. On the basis of the results, the division worked with the SUS to increase the number of concurrent-use programs in the state. Increasing the number and variety of these programs has resulted in thousands of students entering upper division who might not have done so previously because of family or work obligations.

Because the division has valid, reliable electronic data covering more than a decade, it is now possible to track students over an extended period of time. Work done in conjunction with the Achieving the Dream initiative offered an opportunity to determine the impact of tracking for three, four, or six years. The workgroup examining the timeframe issue decided that community college students needed to be tracked for six years no matter the initial enrollment status of the student. This is in contrast to the national Graduation Rate Survey, which is currently limited to three years for students who begin as full-time.

Longitudinal tracking is only one of many ways of examining community college students. However, it poses a unique opportunity to compare and contrast diverse aspects of a college career.

Lessons Learned

Eleven key lessons summarize the experiences of Florida professionals in building a key education data system with emphasis on integrating those systems.

Secure and Maintain Executive Leadership and Commitment. Leadership commitment is an important starting place as states or educational organizations within states consider developing systems that involve data collection on the part of local education agencies, controversial issues, and ground-breaking technologies or processes. Leadership commitment may come in the form of legislative initiative, executive-level commitment, or a local groundswell type of support in which local organizations recognize the value-added of state-level data collection and reporting.

Articulate Goals and Purposes. Articulate the goals and purposes of a state-level education information system, both long-term and short-term, and revisit them as necessary. A long-range vision for the systems should also be articulated. At the same time, it is important to realistically manage expectations. This means that short-range, achievable goals must be clearly outlined. It is never a bad idea to exceed short-term goals.

Articulate Benefits and Risks for Everyone Involved. State level education systems, including integrated ones, have benefits that include reducing and managing the impact of changing federal or state reporting requirements on local entities, ensuring consistent and accurate reporting and analysis, offering a means of reporting state or federal data on behalf of local organizations, and providing comparative information statewide. There are also significant risks. Initial start-up expenses must be borne and accounted for. Data, which are often sensitive, must be collected and protected in a fashion that precludes untoward release or improper use. There may be political and ownership kinds of resistance. Both the benefits and risks must be made clear.

Build on Existing Systems and Expertise. To the extent possible, build on existing systems and expertise. School districts, community colleges, and universities have significant investments and expertise in defining, designing, collecting, maintaining, and reporting data on students, staff, facilities management, and finance. Any state-level development should build on this knowledge and expertise.

Pursue Collaborations and Partnerships. Pursue opportunities to provide service and share information. The collected data are not useful solely for federal and state reporting and accountability processes. They can also serve consumers in making decisions about institutions and academic paths.

They can assist in managing student learning and achievement. They can support research on best practices and promising new policies. These opportunities must be actively sought as part of a system's ongoing operation.

Publicize Products, Services, and Capabilities. All potential and actual reports, analyses, research documents, and other services must be known to users so they will peruse available information and request additional information needed for their purposes.

Ensure Data Integrity. Establish and maintain a culture of data and information integrity. Timely and accurate data are a necessary attribute of any data system. Data quality processes such as reporting edits, data dictionaries, technical assistance, and data audits are a critical part of systems development, implementation, and maintenance.

Adhere to Confidentiality and Release Requirements. Exceed all requirements dealing with confidentiality and restricted release. There are state and federal laws concerning collection and dissemination of individually identifiable student data. The best known is the Family Educational Rights and Privacy Act, also known as FERPA. In integrated systems, laws governing other sources of information complicate the legal requirements. All provisions must be observed and should be exceeded to foster confidence in the system. However, the laws and requirements should not be considered as barriers that preclude any form of data collection or data exchange involving individually identifiable data.

Secure Ongoing Support. Ongoing, reliable support is necessary to maintain the investments in time and money that were made in initial development. Ongoing support should be secured from regular state sources and supplemented with federal or foundation grants or participation in funded research.

Recognize Change Is Constant. Recognize that change is constant; keep ahead of it. Government leadership, from both elected and appointed officials, is constantly changing. Staff below the leadership level change as well. Technology changes, data needs change, and requirements change. To the degree that changes can be anticipated, they should be addressed. Data system professionals need to be prepared to anticipate changes and respond to them as they occur.

It's Never Over. All of these lessons remain relevant over time. They do not lose their relevance after a system is successfully implemented; nor do they end with changes in administration or key staff. They must be constantly addressed.

JAY PFEIFFER *is the deputy commissioner for the Florida Department of Education.*

PATRICIA WINDHAM *is associate vice chancellor for evaluation for the Florida Community College System.*

NEW DIRECTIONS FOR COMMUNITY COLLEGES • DOI: 10.1002/cc

5

This chapter describes the National Student Clearing-house and discusses opportunities and challenges for tracking community college students. It also presents a system perspective on using clearinghouse data to promote more comprehensive student and graduate tracking.

The National Student Clearinghouse: The Largest Current Student Tracking Database

Craig Schoenecker, Richard Reeves

The National Student Clearinghouse (NSC) is a nonprofit organization created in conjunction with the higher education community and the student lending industry to supply enrollment verifications for student borrowers. At its inception in 1993, the NSC furnished only that. However, as its membership increased, the NSC added other services, including a degree verification service and a student tracking service. In 1996, the clearinghouse served more than one thousand institutions, and in 2007 it had more than three thousand member institutions submitting data. Although these institutions constitute less than one-half of the U.S. postsecondary institutions included in the IPEDS survey, they enroll more than 92 percent of the nation's students. The participation rates for two-year and four-year institutions are even higher than the 92 percent figure for all institutions. (Nonmember institutions are typically small trade schools.) This chapter describes the NSC, its student tracking service, and the legal basis for that service. It also describes how a public higher education system has used the service to improve the completeness of its transfer measures and discusses the limitations of NSC student tracking.

Family Educational Rights and Privacy Act

The federal Family Educational Rights and Privacy Act (FERPA) protects the privacy of students' education records. FERPA requires that students give

New Directions for Community Colleges, no. 143, Fall 2008 © 2008 Wiley Periodicals, Inc.
Published online in Wiley InterScience (www.interscience.wiley.com) • DOI: 10.1002/cc.335

consent for the release of information from their education records, except in certain limited circumstances. The act does permit colleges and universities to disclose directory information about students without their consent. Directory information is defined as information that would not be considered harmful if disclosed (FERPA, 2004). However, the institution must notify students regarding the types of information it designates as directory information and allow them to prevent disclosure. Examples of directory information are name, address, telephone number, and date of birth.

The NSC has a service, StudentTracker, which enables member institutions to improve their measurement of educational outcomes by tracking students across institutions using the NSC enrollment and degree database. The clearinghouse does not sell lists of students, and organizations may not request student-level data for students with specific affiliations such as institutional type or geographic location. The NSC operates on a quid-pro-quo policy with all organizations; that is, only institutions that submit their student data are able to use the service and receive student tracking data from the NSC system.

The NSC's StudentTracker has been found to be in compliance with the provisions of FERPA (Rooker, 1999). Submission of directory information data on the part of requesting institutions and the return file from NSC exclude students who have exercised their right to prevent disclosure of directory information. Requesting institutions submit directory information data elements only on students they want to track, and the NSC supplies directory information data elements only in the returned student unit-level file. The NSC further protects the privacy of students by not notifying a requesting institution of changes in student identifying information via StudentTracker.

Content and Analysis of StudentTracker Files. The StudentTracker file contains student identifying data elements, data on the institution at which the student is enrolled, dates of enrollment, degrees earned and date of same, and data on major and class standing. NSC data are only as good as the files that participating institutions submit. All valid records submitted by participating institutions are loaded into the NSC system. Some idiosyncrasies related to individual institutions are passed on in the StudentTracker files. Two examples are the *enrollment begin* and *enrollment end* dates, which are term-specific. The dates reflect a variety of term types: semester, trimester, quarter, periodic. The StudentTracker file has one record for each term of enrollment for each student at each institution. If a student's enrollment status (full-time or part-time) changes during a term, a second record will be included in the return file, reflecting the new enrollment status and the date associated with the change. The beginning and ending dates enable one to distinguish the respective duration of each enrollment status within the terms. Some have suggested that the NSC collect information for terms, but the heterogeneity of term policies in higher education makes such a change undesirable. Problems also arise when data are unnecessarily categorized, and it is generally best to have more information rather than less. Furnishing term beginning

NEW DIRECTIONS FOR COMMUNITY COLLEGES • DOI: 10.1002/cc

and ending dates enables researchers to examine enrollment overlap, duration, or other continuous measures over time.

StudentTracker files are returned in a spreadsheet file format and must be converted to another format for analysis. The NSC developed code sets for SPSS and SAS to assist researchers in importing and classifying StudentTracker files. Researchers are encouraged to use these files and share any code they have developed with NSC so it can be shared with other StudentTracker users.

New users of StudentTracker files often summarize the file into a "one record per student" format with each term of enrollment enumerated as a new set of variables. This practice often creates more problems than it solves. The recommended method is to import all records as they are returned. The next step is to create new variables that fit the condition of interest (for example, enrollment in 2008) and summarize the data file by student and condition. This approach produces the desired one record per student while preserving the term records.

Certain research questions require matching of the NSC school codes with other datasets. The Integrated Postsecondary Education Data System (IPEDS) institutional characteristics data file contains the Office of Postsecondary Education ID number (OPEID) and the IPEDS unique identifier (UNITID). This file can be used as a crosswalk to match the NSC school codes to the OPEID and the UNITID in IPEDS data files in order to add other data to an analysis. Common questions such as how many students choose to attend institutions with higher graduation rates, lower costs of attendance, or with different geographic environments can be addressed with this approach.

The NSC StudentTracker service offers institutions and systems the opportunity to substantially expand the completeness of their transfer measures and reporting. The next section of the chapter describes and quantifies the advantages and limitations experienced by the Minnesota State Colleges and Universities system in using the service.

Minnesota State Colleges and Universities

The Minnesota State Colleges and Universities system comprises thirty community and technical colleges and seven state universities. It enrolls 240,000 students annually in credit courses with 135,000 full-time equivalents and another 135,000 students in noncredit courses. The system has 34,000 annual graduates and programs that range from one-semester occupational certificates to applied doctorates.

The system was created in 1995 through the merger of three separate public higher education systems. The community college, technical college, and state university systems were placed under the authority of a single governing board and chancellor. A primary rationale for creating the system was to increase and improve student transfer.

Student Tracking Initiatives. The Minnesota State Colleges and University system participated in several initiatives to expand its student tracking capabilities. The key step was the decision to create a comprehensive integrated record system. This records system has been used since 1999 by all thirty-seven colleges and universities and supports the admissions, student records, financial aid, accounts receivable, curriculum, finance, and human resource functions. A data warehouse serves as a repository for comprehensive records of students enrolled at a system college or university. Finally, the system submits an annual data file on its students to the Minnesota Office of Higher Education for inclusion in a statewide student unit record database. Although the system's data allowed comprehensive tracking within and among its institutions, there were substantial gaps in tracking students who transferred out of the system.

Transfer Out of the System. System colleges have traditionally been a significant source of transfers to the University of Minnesota and private colleges and universities in the state. The statewide student database offers limited tracking of this activity; it captures only fall enrollment records for the public and most of the private colleges and universities in the state.

Interstate Tuition Reciprocity. The state's interstate tuition reciprocity agreements with North Dakota, South Dakota, and Wisconsin result in enrollment of more than twenty thousand Minnesota residents annually at public colleges and universities in these three states (Minnesota Office of Higher Education, 2007). Student unit record data on the state residents enrolled in these states, however, are not integrated with the Office of Higher Education's statewide student database.

Summary Reporting. Finally, as a result of state data privacy provisions the Office of Higher Education supplies only summary information on the number of transfer students enrolled at Minnesota institutions, rather than student unit record data.

Expanded Student Tracking. To address these limitations and respond to a board of trustees accountability initiative for expanded transfer reporting, the system expanded its student tracking in 2002. System leadership decided that all of its institutions would participate in the NSC core, degree verify, enrollment verify, and StudentTracker services. Although system institutions were using the NSC core service, only a few were using the other services.

Uses of NSC StudentTracker. A high rate of NSC participation in the region meant that StudentTracker had the potential to improve the system's student tracking. An analysis of IPEDS fall 2005 headcount and current NSC participation indicated that 94 percent of students in Minnesota and its four bordering states were enrolled at NSC participating institutions. Participation was highest at public (99 percent) and private institutions (92 percent) and substantially lower at for-profit institutions (49 percent).

The Minnesota system has made a practice of offering a range of research and reporting services for its colleges and universities. The addition of the NSC StudentTracker data represented an extension of this practice. Working in consultation with college and university institutional researchers, system staff developed standard methodologies for analysis of the NSC data and for its integration with other system datasets. Reporting includes institutional results and contextual information on results for other system institutions.

The NSC StudentTracker data are used within the system for several reporting and research projects and at many colleges and universities for institutional analyses. System uses include longitudinal tracking of entering student cohorts and calculation of transfers for the IPEDS graduation rate survey. NSC data also are used to generate more comprehensive reporting on transfer out of system institutions. Finally, responses to the system standard graduate follow-up survey are supplemented with NSC data. The longitudinal tracking and student transfer projects are discussed in more detail to illustrate the benefits and limitations of using NSC student data.

Longitudinal Tracking: Student Persistence and Completion Rate

The system's institutional research (IR) directors group was charged to develop a set of accountability measures for the board of trustees in 2003. The IR group developed a measure similar to the student advancement rate that had been recommended by the Joint Commission on Accountability Reporting (JCAR). The system measure, called the persistence and completion rate, uses the JCAR calculation but is reported more frequently than the JCAR recommendations and is reported for all entering students. The JCAR advancement rate was defined as the number of students in a cohort enrolled plus the number who graduated or transferred divided by the total number in the cohort (AASCU, 1996). The total persistence and completion rate as well as enrolled or retained, graduated, and transferred components are reported for cohorts of fall entering students at each of the eleven subsequent fall and spring semesters during the six years after entry.

All fall entering students are included in the cohort but are classified into one of five subcohorts for purposes of reporting: undergraduate first-time, undergraduate transfer, high school, nondegree seeking, and graduate students. The rate is also reported with breakouts for several student characteristics, among them full-time or part-time status, ethnicity, Perkins program eligibility, first-generation status, and Pell grant status.

NSC StudentTracker data along with system enrollment and graduation data are used to update the persistence and completion measure twice annually. StudentTracker batch submission files are created from the system's student database with SPSS. The returned StudentTracker spreadsheet files are converted back to database format with SPSS. The resulting database files include all of the returned NSC data elements and all of the returned records. The typical StudentTracker submission file for the measure includes approximately 400,000 students in six recent entering cohorts. The NSC returns approximately 1.5 million enrollment records for the submitted students.

Table 5.1. Students and Records Returned by NSC Student Tracker

Entry Term	Cohort Sent	Students Returned	Percentage Students Returned	Records Returned	Records per Student	Institutions Returned
Fall 2000	64,978	46,459	71%	313,516	7	1,259
Fall 2001	67,759	46,587	69%	300,221	6	1,226
Fall 2002	68,789	48,254	70%	294,557	6	1,121
Fall 2003	70,033	47,672	68%	263,169	6	1,028
Fall 2004	67,742	46,410	69%	211,609	5	950
Fall 2005	67,416	46,375	69%	156,869	3	729
Total	406,717	281,757	69%	1,539,941	5	1,832

Note: Unique institutions between fall 2000 and 2005.

Table 5.1 presents information on students and records from a system StudentTracker submission.

The StudentTracker return file contained records for 70 percent of the students in the submission file. There are two reasons that 30 percent of the submitted students were not returned. First, student date of birth is used in the StudentTracker process to confirm matches of submitted student records with the NSC student database. Because twenty-three of the thirty-seven system colleges and universities do not designate date of birth as directory information, it cannot be included in the StudentTracker submission file for students from those institutions. In addition, approximately 5 percent of system students do not report their date of birth. When date of birth is not given and a submitted student record matches more than one student in the NSC database, no match is reported in the returned file. Second, because 2 percent of the students did not report their social security number to the college or university in which they enrolled, they were not loaded in the NSC database.

The StudentTracker file returned by the NSC contained 1.5 million student enrollment records from 1,832 higher education institutions, as shown in Table 5.1. Students from the earlier entering cohorts who have been tracked for longer periods of time had more enrollment records and were attending more institutions than students from more recent cohorts. The average number of enrollment records ranged from seven for students in the fall 2000 cohort to three for students in the fall 2005 cohort. The number of institutions ranged from 1,259 for the fall 2000 cohort to 729 for the fall 2005 cohort. The 1,832 institutions had 2,084 reporting units. Some institutions report enrollment records to NSC using different institution codes to distinguish separate reporting units such as campuses or undergraduate and graduate units.

NEW DIRECTIONS FOR COMMUNITY COLLEGES • DOI: 10.1002/cc

Analysis and Impact of NSC Data

The NSC StudentTracker records along with system enrollment and graduation records are used to determine each student's status during the eleven semesters after entry. System enrollment and graduation records for the institution the student entered are used to create retention and graduation flags for up to eleven semesters after entry. System and NSC enrollment records are used to create transfer flags for up to eleven fall and spring semesters after entry. Because students may have more than one flag set for a given semester (such as both graduated and transferred) each student is assigned to a single status according to the hierarchy of graduated, retained, and transferred.

Use of the NSC StudentTracker service enables the system to identify substantially more students as transfers. Table 5.2 presents information on the additional transfer students identified through StudentTracker. System transfers were identified using the system's enrollment records and ranged from 17 percent of the fall 2005 cohort to 29 percent of the fall 2000 cohort. The NSC transfers include students who were not identified in system enrollment records but were identified as transfers through StudentTracker. The NSC service identified an additional 12 percent of the students in the cohort as transfers and raised transfers to 37 percent. StudentTracker increased the number of transfer students identified by an average of 47 percent.

Romano and Wisniewski (2005) reported that NSC tracking more than doubled the number of transfer students identified for two community colleges in New York. The increase was compared to tracking that was done using a more limited State University of New York transfer tracking system. The smaller NSC gain reported for the Minnesota system is likely due to the system's more comprehensive record system, which identified more transfer students prior to the NSC tracking.

Completeness of NSC Student Tracking. Exclusion of birth date from student records in an NSC submission file substantially reduces the

Table 5.2. Additional Transfers Identified with NSC Tracking

Entry Term	Cohort Sent	Percentage System Transfers	Percentage NSC Transfer	Percentage Total Transfers	Percentage Increase Transfers
Fall 2000	64,978	29%	14%	43%	49%
Fall 2001	67,759	27%	13%	40%	46%
Fall 2002	68,789	27%	13%	40%	47%
Fall 2003	70,033	26%	12%	38%	45%
Fall 2004	67,742	23%	11%	34%	49%
Fall 2005	67,416	17%	8%	25%	47%
Total	406,717	25%	12%	37%	47%

completeness of resulting student tracking. The twenty-three system colleges and universities that do not designate date of birth as directory information account for 59 percent of the students submitted in the search. Two-thirds of the within-system transfers were found in the NSC file for institutions that designate date of birth as directory information; only 38 percent of within-system transfers were found in the NSC file for institutions that do not designate date of birth as directory information. Systemwide, 46 percent of the within-system transfers were found in the NSC file for the earliest cohort and 59 percent for the most recent cohort.

Although use of the StudentTracker service has enabled the Minnesota system to identify substantially more transfer students, the less complete tracking without date of birth is an important limitation. If this within-system analysis is indicative of tracking completeness outside of the system, the overall percentage NSC transfers of 12 percent in Table 5.2 could be understated by as much as 50 percent. If this were the case, the actual percentage of total transfers (37 percent in Table 5.2) could be as high as 47 percent. These results should not be viewed as a reason to designate student date of birth as directory information. The increasing incidence of identity theft and aggressive marketing to students are compelling reasons for colleges and universities to designate a more limited set of data elements as directory information.

Uses of the Persistence and Completion Measure. The persistence and completion measure is used for several purposes at the system and institution levels. The measure is reported for each institution in the system's board of trustees dashboard. The board also approved system and institution targets in 2006 for improvements in retention and for improvements in the overall persistence and completion rates for students of color. The colleges and universities use the measure to assess the impact of initiatives to improve retention and graduation rates. The measure is also reported in an interactive Web-based analytic tool and in a student-level data file.

Improving Student Transfer Tracking with NSC Data

Tracking student transfer has been a priority for the Minnesota system, because it includes both two-year and four-year institutions and because improving transfer was a primary reason for its creation. The integrated record system supplies a rich source of data for tracking student transfer into and among the state colleges and universities. The availability of data on student courses accepted in transfer, combined with students' course and term enrollment data, has enabled the system to develop extensive tracking and reporting on transfer. Reporting for each college and university includes the number of transfer students, records and credits sent and received, the success of transfer students compared to nontransfer students, and the number and percentage of earned credits accepted in transfer.

NEW DIRECTIONS FOR COMMUNITY COLLEGES • DOI: 10.1002/cc

The use of NSC StudentTracker data in addition to data from its student records has enabled the system to improve the completeness of its transfer reporting. Prior to adding NSC data, the system reported an annual average of 11,518 students transferring from one system college or university to another between fiscal year 2000 and 2005. StudentTracker identified an additional 17,711 students, on average, who transferred from one of its colleges or universities to an institution outside the system. The NSC data indicated that transfers to nonsystem institutions are increasing more rapidly than transfers to system institutions, going from 57 percent of outgoing transfer in 2000 to 63 percent in 2005. The addition of the NSC data increased the number of identified outgoing transfer students by an average of 153 percent between 2000 and 2005. This increase in the number of outgoing transfer students may be due in part to the increased participation of Minnesota institutions in NSC during this time period.

Limitations of NSC Database

Although the advantages of using the NSC system are apparent, the NSC's database of students does have some limiting factors that affect student tracking. The limitations include its treatment of students without social security numbers and international students, the extent of information available through the service, and the fact that some institutions do not participate in the NSC core service.

Currently, only students with valid social security numbers are loaded into the database. This limitation has to do with the origins of the NSC being related to student loan verification. Because international students do not have a social security number or a unique ID that is permanent, they also are excluded from the NSC database. In 2007, the NSC added the capacity to receive and serve international students from collegiate institutions. It is unclear, however, if this added service will result in international students' being matched in StudentTracker.

Although the NSC database contains records for 92 percent of U.S. higher education students, the StudentTracker data are available only to institutions participating in the core service. An institution that does not participate in the DegreeVerify service does not receive degree data through StudentTracker. Similarly, an institution that does not submit the expanded data elements does not receive them in StudentTracker.

Another important limitation of NSC data is the fact that some institutions do not participate, and consequently it is not possible to track students at these institutions. Unlike a survey, which may have a low response rate but allow all possible outcomes, the NSC data have missing data that cannot be weighted to reflect an estimated rate. Researchers should be aware of and cite the NSC participation rate as a limitation. Additionally, institutions rarely submit enrollment data for prior terms when they sign up for the core service. In contrast, they often send all available degree records for the DegreeVerify service. Ninety-six percent of Minnesota's students attended NSC participating institutions in 2005. In 2000, the NSC had less than 70 percent of Minnesota's students in the core service. Such a dramatic increase in participation over a short period of time is characteristic of most states. The NSC furnishes a list of participating institutions that can assist in assessing participation (NSC, 2007).

Next Steps in Student Tracking

The clearinghouse has initiated several activities to improve NSC student tracking and available data. Several data elements have been added to the core service data submission. Some of the additional elements will be used to improve student tracking and others will offer additional information to NSC members. NSC has also undertaken a study to estimate eventual degree attainment by students using its student and degree databases.

The Minnesota system has also undertaken steps to improve the completeness of its NSC tracking and make the information more easily accessible to its colleges and universities. Subsequent degree attainment by system students at nonsystem institutions will be tracked with the StudentTracker degree verify data. The persistence and completion rate will be revised to distinguish between students who transfer and those who transfer and graduate. Approaches for improving the completeness of student tracking when student date of birth is not directory information are also being considered. Finally, the system will integrate the NSC student tracking data into a data warehouse to streamline access by its colleges and universities.

Conclusions

There are substantive advantages in using the National Student Clearinghouse to improve student tracking. The Minnesota system experience suggests that NSC tracking can increase the students in a cohort that are found to be transfers by 47 percent, compared to tracking with its student records. Transfers of system students to nonsystem institutions identified by the NSC represented 61 percent of outgoing transfers. The use of NSC student data by a system also offers the advantages of consistent methodologies, integration with other datasets, and reporting of contextual information.

The advantages of using the NSC data to improve student tracking must be tempered with knowledge of the limitations inherent in the data and processing. The legal framework used for the StudentTracker service can lead to substantial underreporting of transfer students for institutions that do not designate date of birth as directory information. The NSC database excludes students for whom no social security number has been submitted, including international students. Finally, the StudentTracker service gives information only to institutions that submit data to the NSC.

NEW DIRECTIONS FOR COMMUNITY COLLEGES • DOI: 10.1002/cc

References

American Association of State Colleges and Universities (AASCU). *JCAR Technical Conventions Manual.* Washington, D.C.: American Association of State Colleges and Universities, 1996.

Family Educational Rights and Privacy Act. 34 C.F.R. Part 99 (2004).

Minnesota Office of Higher Education. *Tuition Reciprocity Data Overview.* St. Paul: Minnesota Office of Higher Education, 2007.

National Student Clearinghouse. *Core Participants.* Herndon, Va.: National Student Clearinghouse, 2007.

Romano, R. M., and Wisniewski, M. "Tracking Community College Transfers Using National Student Clearinghouse Data." *AIR Professional File,* 2005, *94,* 1–11.

Rooker, L. S. *Family Policy Compliance.* Washington, D.C.: U.S. Department of Education, 1999. http://www.ed.gov/policy/gen/guid/fpco/ferpa/library/herndonva.html (accessed May 31, 2008).

CRAIG SCHOENECKER *is system director for research for the Minnesota State Colleges and Universities System.*

RICHARD REEVES *is director of research for the National Student Clearinghouse.*

NEW DIRECTIONS FOR COMMUNITY COLLEGES • DOI: 10.1002/cc

6

The Washington State Board for Community and Technical Colleges used the findings from a tracking study of low-skill working adults to significantly influence and change state policy and practice for this critical component of the state's workforce.

Tracking Low-Skill Adult Students Longitudinally: Using Research to Guide Policy and Practice

David Prince

Community and technical colleges are vital to their regional economies and the economic well-being of their area residents. With their open doors, two-year colleges are entry ways to postsecondary education for a variety of students. Because community college student groups have differing needs, it is important to understand the diverse student populations these institutions serve. Student age is one of the most important distinguishing characteristics that colleges should account for; traditional college-age students tend to have different enrollment patterns and academic support needs than older students do (Calcagno, Crosta, Bailey, and Jenkins, 2007). Within these age groupings, colleges should assess the needs in their communities for high school students concurrently enrolled in college, recent high school graduates, and older adult populations with a range of prior learning and attainment (McGuinness and Jones, 2003).

For the past several years, the Washington State Board for Community and Technical Colleges has conducted applied research to inform and develop policies for increasing educational attainment and narrowing educational

Note: The state board wishes to acknowledge assistance and support from these organizations for much of the work cited in this paper: the Ford Foundation's Bridges to Opportunity Initiative, Jobs for the Future, Achieve the Dream and the Washington State College Spark Foundation, and Columbia University's Community College Research Center.

NEW DIRECTIONS FOR COMMUNITY COLLEGES, no. 143, Fall 2008 © 2008 Wiley Periodicals, Inc.
Published online in Wiley InterScience (www.interscience.wiley.com) • DOI: 10.1002/cc.336

disparities in the state. In 2004, the board used student unit record data systems to conduct a longitudinal tracking study of adults attending community and technical colleges as first-time students with little or no prior postsecondary education. Most of the new students that were studied entered the college system through the literacy door for noncredit adult basic education. Washington State's community and technical colleges offer adult basic education for students with reading or math skills at less than a ninth grade level, lacking a high school diploma, or needing English as a second language (ESL). These programs may be organized within other departments in some colleges. But regardless of where they are housed, they typically function separately, with little connection to the rest of the college. The board wanted to know how these students fared beyond adult basic education (ABE). Did they move on to college credit instruction? What were their experiences in the labor market after attending? How much did they earn after leaving the college system?

The study findings went on to spark new dialogue in state government, in the state's higher education and workforce training policy boards, and on college campuses. This chapter describes the study and how its findings resulted in new policies and practices. It concludes with a discussion of how the state board is using research and data to increase achievement among all students by developing a new performance and improvement measurement system.

The Changing Economy and Changing Demographics

The need for at least some postsecondary education is nearly universal in today's economy. Policy makers are increasingly focused on how to improve postsecondary access and success for expanded segments of society. It is difficult to find an article or study that does not directly link postsecondary success with economic competitiveness for the country and the individual's economic well-being. Increases in educational requirements for gainful employment juxtaposed with changing demographics require that we increase educational attainment in broad segments of the population, or pay the consequences for having too few skilled workers.

There is also a wage premium for well-educated workers. Although a high school diploma was once enough to secure a decent living, increasing education and skill requirements make this far more difficult, widening the divide between those who have an education and those who do not (Carnevale and Desrochers, 2003). For example, a worker in Washington state with some college will earn on average $4,500 a year more than one with a high school diploma and better than $12,000 a year more than those without a high school diploma. The education premium is estimated to have contributed to one-quarter of total earnings growth for Washington workers between 1990 and 2000 (Gardner, 2005).

So, do Washington's workers have the skills they need for the state to be competitive? Where will tomorrow's workforce come from? Many analysts point out that tomorrow's workforce will come largely from today's workers, because not all of the demands for skilled workers with college certificates and degrees can be met solely by preparing new young entrants to the workforce (Bailey and Mingle, 2003). In Washington State, there are 1.4 million adults twenty-five and older who do not have any education beyond high school. Over the next ten years, the fastest-growing age group will be adults twenty-five to thirty-five years old. Four in ten of these prime-working-age adults have at most some college; three in ten have a high school diploma or less, a number that is on par with the combined size of Washington's next ten high school graduating classes.

Persons of color are the fastest-growing demographic groups in Washington State. The two fastest-growing segments are Asians and Hispanics. The former will grow as a segment of the workforce from 9 to 15 percent, the latter from 6 to 14 percent. Together they will constitute nearly six in every ten new labor force participants between 2000 and 2030.

College-level attainment of African Americans, Latinos, and Native Americans falls far below the level required to stay competitive. In Washington state, nearly half of Latino adults have less than a high school education. More Native American adults have less than a high school education than have an associate degree or higher. A higher proportion of African American adults have a high school education or less, and a smaller percentage have a baccalaureate degree or higher compared to whites. Growth in non-English-speaking adults adds to the challenges; there has been a doubling in the state of adults with limited English between 1990 and 2000. Nearly half of non-English-speaking adults in Washington have a high school education or less (Lasater and Elliott, 2005). To respond to the demographic shifts under way, Washington state will have to train and educate incumbent workers and older working-age adults so that they are able to maximize the opportunities afforded to them and so the state's workforce will remain competitive. One of the most critical policy questions policy makers can ask is how well the state prepares students along the continuum of education programs or pathways beyond high school.

Education Attainment and Earnings for Low-Skill Adult Students

The Washington state two-year college system comprises twenty-nine community and five technical colleges. The system has a threefold mission of adult literacy, workforce education, and transfer preparation for the first two years of college. The colleges enroll some 163,000 full-time equivalent (FTE) students (460,000 headcount) in an academic year. Eighty percent of the FTEs are supported by state funding and student tuition. Seventeen percent are funded through contracts with government agencies and employers, and the others are self-supporting.

The community and technical colleges' data systems generate student unit record data on enrollment, transcripts, and financial aid that allow the state board to track students as they attend any college within the system. The system can link student records to other state systems for matches with records on employment, welfare participation, and enrollment at the state's public four-year institutions. For many years, the state board has tracked the success of students in advancing to higher levels of education, transferring to baccalaureate programs, and moving into the labor market, among other outcomes. In 2005, the board undertook a descriptive analysis of the working-age adult student population who were entering the community college system and had at most a high school education. The full study, *Building Pathways to Success for Low-Skill Adult Students: Lessons for Community College Policy and Practice from a Statewide Longitudinal Tracking Study* (Prince and Jenkins, 2005), is available through the Community College Research Center.

The data used for the analysis contained unit records for nearly thirty-five thousand students who were new to the system in 1996–97 and 1998–99. These adult working-age students represented about one-third of all new Washington community and technical college students. Nearly half of the students were in the fast-growing twenty-five-to-thirty-five age segment of the population. Another 15 percent of the students were younger adults between eighteen and twenty-four with no high school diploma or GED. This younger population was included because, by dropping out of high school, they had in effect entered the adult labor force. The remaining students were between the ages of thirty-five and forty-nine—adults in their prime working years. The students reflected the growing diversity in the state's population. One-half were persons of color; Latinos accounted for more than one-fourth of the students.

Not surprisingly for adults with at most a high school education, the students in the cohorts were predominantly from low-income backgrounds. This determination was based on using data from three sources: employment earnings before the students entered college from a match with state employment records, receipt of public assistance from a match with state welfare records, and place of residence using student zip code address and census data for family income in those zip codes.

The students were classified by their starting level of education. Students who enrolled in at least one ESL class in their first two years were classified as starting in ESL. Students who enrolled in ABE or GED instruction were classified as less than high school. Three-fourths of the students in the cohorts entered through one of these literacy doors, 35 percent as ESL and 40 percent as less than high school. Of the remaining students, three-fourths enrolled in college-credit workforce programs, while the others enrolled in transfer preparation programs. Their starting level of education was classified as high school or GED to start, on the basis of their admission records.

The study followed the students in the Washington community and technical college system for five years and then measured their earnings in the sixth year. Compared with students who earned fewer than ten college credits, those who took at least one year's worth of college-credit courses and earned a certificate or a degree had an average annual earnings advantage of $7,000 for students who started in ESL and $8,500 for those who started at less than high school.

These findings are consistent with previous research on the economic returns to a subbaccalaureate education, which has found that the wage gains associated with postsecondary education of less than a year are negligible (Bailey, Kienzl, and Marcotte, 2004; Grubb, 2002; Kienzl, 2004). Other research on Washington State's workforce shows that workers with college education and training have substantially higher lifetime earnings than do those with no college, and these workers are also in higher demand among employers (Spaulding, Seppanen, and Wilson, 2006).

Reaching the Tipping Point

The study found a substantial difference in earnings between students who completed one year or more of college plus a credential and those who did not make it to that tipping point. However, relatively few students reached this milestone. For ESL and ABE students, the study found that nearly eight in ten go no further than noncredit basic skills, at most making modest gains or earning a GED. Two out of three starting with a GED left with less than one year of college credit completed. For those starting with a high school diploma, six in ten left with less, and some a lot less, than one year completed. Table 6.1 presents the highest education attainment on the basis of students' education when they first enrolled.

In the study, having or earning a high school diploma or GED was critical to students' going further. Upwards of two-thirds of the ESL and a slightly larger number of high school students who went beyond noncredit ABE to college workforce education and training had a secondary credential. ESL students most likely earned this high school diploma in their country of origin. Having a high school credential made receiving financial aid more likely. It also increased the chances that students would continue to build their college readiness with developmental instruction, the next level of remediation in the state system. Receiving financial aid and taking developmental courses made it two to three times more likely for a student to reach the tipping point. Another factor associated with higher attainment was if a student intended to stay for a year or longer. However, even though all these factors were clearly advantageous, only one-third of the ABE and ESL students who went on to college-level instruction received financial aid or took a development course.

A larger group of students also started in ABE and ESL with a high school diploma or GED in hand but never went beyond noncredit studies.

Table 6.1. Highest Educational Attainment After Five Years of Washington State Community and Technical Colleges: First-Time College Students Who Started with a High School Education or Less in 1996–97 or 1997–98

| | Starting Education Level | | | |
Five-Year Highest Attainment	ESL	HS (ABE)	GED	Less Than HS Diploma
Number of students	12,396	13,925	2,199	6,438
Noncredits	87%	61%	13%	1%
GED	0%	8%	—	—
Plan*	1%	1%	3%	3%
< 10 college credits	7%	16%	28%	19%
10–44 college credits	2%	7%	26%	32%
45+ college credits	1%	2%	12%	13%
Less than one-year certificate	1%	1%	3%	4%
Certificate of one year or more	1%	2%	5%	6%
Associate degree	1%	1%	9%	12%

Note: *Plan refers to students who completed a typically short-term course of training or education prescribed by another state agency such as the Department of Social and Health Services or a One-Stop Center.

Of further note, almost no ESL students who were lacking their high school credential earned a GED during the five-year period the study followed them. Hispanic students were least likely to go beyond ESL. They were half as likely as other students to go further, even if they had their high school diploma. Hispanic males were far less likely than females to do so.

Using Study Findings as a Catalyst for Change

The potential for adult basic education students to move beyond ABE would seem strong given that these programs are offered by the two-year system. However, the research showed that relatively few students transition to postsecondary education and training. If they do transition, it is often to training for jobs on the lowest rung on the ladder, with few advancing beyond to higher wages and high-skill jobs. Often, the training they receive is not aligned in pathways but based on a patchwork of credit and noncredit courses. This is because Washington State community and technical colleges have not had strong coordination or partnering among the three mission areas (basic skills, workforce, and transfer) to facilitate bridging or transitioning of students from one mission area to the next; nor has the state had policies that encourage colleges to align their mission areas to create seamless transitions.

The study findings suggested that community colleges need to rethink and redesign policies and practices in order for more low-skill adults to

NEW DIRECTIONS FOR COMMUNITY COLLEGES • DOI: 10.1002/cc

reach the one-year college-credit milestone. One way to do this is for colleges to think of themselves along the lines of a transit system. If this transit system ran on the schedule of working adults, it could accommodate lots of on-and-off traffic and make connections to further destinations. It could furnish a clear map of the route that adult students might follow to advance in their job and pursue further education, indicating where they can stop out of education for a time and reenter as their circumstances and resources permit. In such an educational transit system, there could be many relatively short trips, all of them leading to meaningful stops; but the system could be designed for adults to go farther and faster than they do in the current system.

The clearest route system for students in this transit system is a career and education pathway, which can be characterized as a series of interconnected education programs, with a surrounding support system, that lead to higher levels of employment and further education and training over time. Each step on a career pathway is designed explicitly to prepare participants for the next level of employment and education (Jenkins and Spence, 2006).

In Washington, the tipping point research has helped persuade the governor and legislature to allocate increased funding for community college programs, has drawn support from the state's Workforce Education and Training Board, and has led to new conversations and programs on college campuses. This has resulted in a new training model and a new financial aid program, both designed to bring low-skill adults to the tipping point.

The process for rethinking and redesigning programs began in two divisions of the state board that were spurred on by the research to break down their "silo" mission walls and work together. The Office for Adult Basic Education came to realize that employment was the core goal for its students and, with the tipping point understood, saw as well the need for developing transitions and pathways. The Workforce Education Division recognized within the changing demographics that low-skilled adults were a critical part of the state's workforce and that many of these adults were falling through the cracks when they came into the college system.

In spring 2004, the two offices jointly piloted projects at ten colleges. called Integrated Basic Education and Skills Training (I-BEST). The pilots tested the traditional notion that students must first complete all levels of basic education before they can begin workforce training. I-BEST pairs English as a second language and adult basic education instructors and professional-technical instructors in the classroom to concurrently plan curricula, instruction, and shared learning outcomes. Recognizing that the longer it takes to master basic skills the less likely adults are to advance from one stage to the next, I-BEST seeks to increase English language proficiency while offering training and education in workforce skills. Results from the pilots demonstrated that I-BEST students were substantially more likely to earn college credits and complete training than were traditional ESL students during the same time period (Prince and Bloomer, 2005).

I-BEST has gone from the ten pilots to all colleges. Two critical components in I-BEST, pairing instructors in the classroom and coordinating student support, cost more than state board funding policies allow. The benefits shown by the tipping point research for bringing students further and faster in their educational achievement have resulted in increased funding support from the state board and the state legislature. The state board changed its funding approach for I-BEST students to reimburse colleges 1.75 times the standard per student amount after the pilots. The legislature in 2007–2009 budgeted an additional $4.9 million for enhanced I-BEST funding to continue to grow the model and support its extra costs.

The tipping point research has also influenced how the state views financial aid policy. Other analyses by the state board have found that because many working age adults attend part-time and do not necessarily identify themselves as degree-seeking, they are often not eligible (or do not apply) for traditional aid. In 2006, the state's Workforce Training and Education Coordinating Board undertook a study of financial aid and reported to the legislature that financial costs of tuition, fees, and living expenses are the most frequent barrier to student access and completion for workforce education and training programs. The workforce board recommended covering tuition costs for the thirteenth year for low-income students, citing the tipping point research. The legislature has targeted $23 million for Opportunity Grants, a new program of financial aid and enhanced support services for low-income adults to progress along demand career pathways.

Both I-BEST and Opportunity Grants will be studied for their effectiveness compared to traditional means for increasing educational attainment and for enabling students to advance in employment and earnings using the tipping point as a benchmark threshold.

Student Socioeconomic Status: Implications for Measuring Colleges and Understanding Student Access and Success

The lack of information regarding student income and socioeconomic background left a gap in the state board's and colleges' understanding of student access and success. In 2006, the state board undertook another study of the student population, titled *The Socioeconomic Well-Being of Washington State: Who Attends Community and Technical Colleges* (Prince, 2006).

Although it has been possible to analyze student socioeconomic background using income for those students who complete the federal application for financial aid (FAFSA), this represents only a small fraction of the students who attend community and technical colleges. Matching student records to welfare and employment files furnishes information on more students; however, the inconsistency across these methods makes analysis difficult.

The state board, working with the Community College Research Center, constructed a socioeconomic (SES) proxy measure for individual students. Using 1990 and 2000 census data for relatively homogeneous geo-graphic areas known as block groups, an average SES for each block group was determined by statistically combining three specific variables: median household income, educational attainment (percentage of adults with a bach-elor's degree or higher), and occupation (percentage of population sixteen or older employed in professional and managerial jobs; Crosta and others, 2006). Student addresses for academic years 1993–94 and 2001–02 were mapped to the census block groups. Students were classified by the SES quin-tile of the block group to which they mapped. The SES proxy was used to analyze and compare student participation to the state population levels.

For the state's population, the study showed that higher educational attainment became increasingly associated with higher socioeconomic sta-tus from 1990 to 2000. Income and the percentage of people employed in professional and managerial occupations increased along with education. Race was not one of the three variables used in defining SES for purposes of the study, but it still mattered. Hispanics, Native Americans, and African Americans all had lower incomes and less educational attainment than whites or Asians. Non-English speakers were increasingly more likely to fall within the lowest quintile. These findings affirmed demographic changes in the state population that underpinned the tipping point research.

The study revealed two important findings for understanding student attainment. First, the findings showed that persons from lower socio-economic standing were more likely to attend college as older students, delaying direct entry from high school. These are the students we tracked through the tipping point research who attended for ABE, ESL, and work-force education. This finding affirms the necessity to focus on younger adults with less than high school education and other dual programs for high school students. The study also found that there were large socioeconomic differences in the local areas the colleges serve. This finding has implications for rethinking individual college performance and needs in the state system.

Conclusion

Building on the research that has been conducted, the state board and the thirty-four colleges are focusing on raising student achievement through evidence-based planning and decision making. The governor and legisla-ture have established the same goal for the state. They created Washington Learns to conduct a comprehensive review of the state's entire education system. The final report cited the tipping point research and, like the state board's ten-year plan, identified raising attainment for all Washingtonians in the state's overarching goals for a world-class education system.

In support of this critical goal, the state board is going forward with a new student achievement initiative for measuring and financially rewarding colleges for advancing more students to higher levels of attainment. The ini-tiative relies on data that can be used to measure continuous improvement in student achievement directly and in easy-to-communicate ways on the part of the colleges. The measures include all students, without favoring any particular groups but rather in alignment with the state's demographics. They allow colleges their maximum flexibility to improve according to their varied community make-up and circumstances (as shown in the SES profile for each college).

The measures were tested empirically and agreed on by a task force broadly representative of the system in 2006–07. They represent incremental gains students make toward college success and achievement of certificates, degrees, and apprenticeships. Each gain is called a momentum point. There are five momentum points: advancing through ABE or ESL; completing pre-college English and math; earning the first, fifteenth, and thirtieth college-level credits; completing college math or computation courses; and earning a certificate backed by at least one year of college level credit, or a degree, or apprenticeship award.

In 2007–08, the entire system is embarking on a learning year to adopt and become familiar with the new measures. Over the next five years, the measures will be used to track student achievement, help colleges plan improvement strategies, and offer supportive evidence for best practices colleges can share with each other as Washington continues to bring research and data to bear on policy and practice.

References

Bailey, T., Kienzl, G. S., and Marcotte, D. E. *The Return to Sub-Baccalaureate Education: The Effects of Schooling, Credentials, and Program of Study on Economic Outcomes.* New York: Community College Research Center, Teachers College, Columbia University, 2004.

Bailey, A., and Mingle, J. *The Adult Learning Gap: Why States Need to Change Their Policies Toward Adult Learners.* Denver, Colo.: Education Commission of the States, 2003.

Calcagno, J. C., Crosta, P., Bailey, T. R., and Jenkins, D. "Stepping Stones to a Degree: The Impact of Enrollment Pathways and Milestones on Community College Student Success." *Research in Higher Education,* 2007, 48(7), 775–801.

Carnevale, A. P., and Desrochers, D. M. *Standards for What? The Economic Roots of K–16 Reform.* Princeton, N.J.: Educational Testing Service, 2003.

Crosta, P., Leinbach, T., and Jenkins, D. with Prince, D., and Whittaker, D. *Using Census Data to Classify Community College Students by Socioeconomic Status and Community Characteristics.* New York: Community College Research Center, Teachers College, Columbia University, 2006.

Gardner, E. *Change in Educational Distribution and Its Impact on Mean Earnings.* Olympia, Wash.: Office of Financial Management, 2005.

Grubb, W. N. "Learning and Earning in the Middle, Part I: National Studies of Pre-Baccalaureate Education." *Economics of Education Review,* 2002, 21, 299–321.

Jenkins, D., and Spence, C. *The Career Pathways How-to Guide.* New York: Workforce Strategies Center, 2006.

Kienzl, G. S. "The Triple Helix of Education and Earnings: The Effect of Schooling, Work and Pathways on the Economic Outcomes of Community College Students." Unpublished doctoral dissertation, Columbia University, 2004.

Lasater, B., and Elliott, B. *Profiles of the Adult Education Target Population.* Washington D.C.: U.S. Department of Education, 2005.

McGuinness Jr., A., and Jones, D. *Narrowing the Gaps in Educational Attainment Within States: A Policymaker's Guide for Assessing and Responding to Needs for Community College Services.* Boulder, Colo.: Center for Higher Education Management Systems, 2003.

Prince, D. *The Socioeconomic Well-Being of Washington State: Who Attends Community and Technical Colleges.* Olympia, Wash.: State Board for Community and Technical Colleges, 2006.

Prince, D., and Bloomer, T. *I-BEST: A Program Integrating Adult Basic Education and Workforce Training.* Olympia, Wash.: State Board for Community and Technical Colleges, 2005.

Prince, D., and Jenkins, D. *Building Pathways to Success for Low-Skill Adults: Lessons for Community College Policy and Practice from a Statewide Longitudinal Tracking Study.* New York: Community College Research Center, Teachers College, Columbia University, 2005.

Spaulding, R., Seppanen, L., and Wilson, B. *A Skilled and Educated Workforce: An Assessment of the Number and Type of Education and Training Credentials Required to Meet Employer Demand.* Olympia, Wash.: State Board for Community and Technical Colleges, 2006.

Workforce Education and Training Board. *Workforce Education Financial Aid and Student Access and Retention. Report to Washington State Legislature.* Olympia, Wash.: Workforce Education and Training Board, 2006.

DAVID PRINCE *is assistant director for research at the Washington State Board for Community and Technical Colleges.*

NEW DIRECTIONS FOR COMMUNITY COLLEGES • DOI: 10.1002/cc

7

This chapter examines lessons learned by states that are using student unit record (SUR) data to improve outcomes for community college students and recommends steps states can take to strengthen their use of SUR databases to benefit students and communities.

Using State Student Unit Record Data to Increase Community College Student Success

Peter Ewell, Davis Jenkins

Most of the data about postsecondary education collected at the state level are used for compliance and accountability. Decisions about what data are tracked and how they are used are dictated mostly by funding requirements, not by a broader vision of the desired outcomes for students and the needs of the communities and regions in which they live. As a result, efforts by higher education institutions and agencies to improve student success or enhance responsiveness to economic and social needs are often undertaken without the benefit of the knowledge that could be gained through analysis of the data they are required to collect.

Fortunately, a growing number of states are recognizing the potential of using data collected at the state level to inform changes in policy and practice that can lead to improved outcomes for students and regions. Particularly potent for this purpose are state-level student unit record (SUR) data, which allow tracking of individual students over time, both within and across education systems and into the labor market. A recent fifty-state survey found that forty states have SUR databases for their public higher education institutions (Ewell and Boeke, 2007). These databases encompass information on 81 percent of the nation's total headcount enrollment in public and private institutions.

In several states with postsecondary SUR systems, state community college agencies are taking the lead in using SUR data to better understand patterns of student progression, identify barriers to student achievement, and

formulate and evaluate strategies for overcoming those barriers. States' efforts to use SUR data for improvement can motivate colleges to undertake similar research using their own data and furnish templates for college-level analyses. Examples of such efforts in Florida and Washington are presented in other chapters of this volume.

This chapter examines lessons learned by states that are using SUR databases to improve outcomes for community college students. It also examines barriers to states' using data for improvement and recommends steps states can take to strengthen their use of SUR data to benefit students and communities.

The chapter is based on our work with eleven states involved in an effort to better use SUR data to improve access and attainment by disadvantaged students at community colleges. Known as the State Data and Community College Student Success Project, this effort is designed to increase use of data by states and colleges to improve student success, develop common performance indicators that focus on student outcomes, create an ongoing forum for collaborative efforts to strengthen state data systems and data uses, and build policy-maker support for strengthening state data collection and applied research capacity. These states—Colorado, Connecticut, Florida, Kentucky, Louisiana, New Mexico, North Carolina, Ohio, Texas, Virginia, and Washington—are participants in one or both of two major national initiatives: the Community College Bridges to Opportunity initiative, which is funded by the Ford Foundation; and Achieving the Dream: Community Colleges Count, which is supported by Lumina Foundation for Education and other funders. A central principle of both initiatives is the importance of using longitudinal unit record data collected at the college and state levels to motivate and guide efforts to improve community college student outcomes.

In 2005, teams led by the National Center for Higher Education Management Systems (NCHEMS) visited community college agencies in the eleven states to conduct data audits designed to assess the capacity of each to collect and analyze community college SUR data, and to examine the potential of developing common performance indicators that would allow benchmarking across states. The resulting report (Ewell, 2006) assessed the feasibility of establishing common indicators and proposing definitions of alternative sets of indicators for states to consider. Teams from the participating states met in San Antonio in January 2006 to discuss Ewell's report and explore possibilities for collaboration. Since that time, the Community College Research Center has worked with several of the participating states to conduct research on student success and institutional effectiveness using SUR data. Additionally, Jobs for the Future has organized a group of community college researchers from states involved with Achieving the Dream. This group is piloting a set of common indicators using data from their states. NCHEMS continues to advise these and other states on how to develop SUR systems and use SUR data strategically.

The next section summarizes some of the lessons learned by states that are using SUR data to improve outcomes for community college students.

The section after that describes some of the challenges involved in using SUR data in these ways. The final section recommends how states can strength their use of data to enhance student success.

Lessons from States That Use Community College SUR Data for Improvement

Site visits to eleven states revealed a number of practical lessons about how longitudinal data systems can and should be used to inform improvements in community college student success.

Lesson One. Efforts to collect and use data both within and among states should be driven by the questions states want to answer, which in turn should be guided by the strategic goals and outcomes they hope to achieve.

SUR data can be used to answer a range of policy questions of interest to higher education institutions, state agencies, and policy makers:

- What percentage of those entering a community college enroll for a second year of study?
- What percentage of those entering a community college ultimately earn a credential (degree or certificate)—whether from the initial college or another institution?
- What percentage of those entering a community college transfer to another institution to pursue bachelor's level study, and how many earn a degree?
- How long does it take students to achieve these objectives?
- How are the experiences of different kinds of students (students from varying demographic groups, attending full-time or part-time, participating in financial aid and student assistance programs, from multiple geographic regions) similar or different in achieving successful outcomes?
- What is the relation between student placement test scores, their actual enrollment in remedial or developmental courses, and their performance in college-level courses?
- How effective is developmental study in preparing students with assessed academic deficiencies for college-level work?
- How effective are adult basic skills programs in enabling participants to take the next step in their education?
- How important to student success are particular academic experiences or attainment of particular milestones (completing twelve or more credits of college-level work in the first year of study)?
- What are the labor market returns for particular credentials, milestones achieved, and course experiences?

Because states' resources for research on questions such as these are likely to be scarce, it is critical that states prioritize their research activities on the basis of their core mission and functions. To help focus research questions on their strategic priorities, states have found it useful to develop a concise storyline statement of their strategic goals. These storylines derive

NEW DIRECTIONS FOR COMMUNITY COLLEGES • DOI: 10.1002/cc

from a strategic analysis by each state of how it could help disadvantaged community college students better achieve success in college and career. Associated with each storyline are a set of priority research questions the given state identified as being important. Using storylines, any state or community college district can develop an easy-to-communicate way to mobilize support for using data and research to promote continuous improvement in how they address the needs of students. Sample storylines formulated by some of the states participating in the State Data and Community College Student Success Project are shown in Exhibit 7.1.

Exhibit 7.1. Sample Strategic Storyline Statements and Associated Research Questions from States Involved in the Community College Data and Student Success Initiative

Colorado

Storyline statement:
Community colleges are the key to solving the "Colorado paradox"—the fact that Colorado has one of the most highly educated workforces, yet one of the lowest college-going rates of native students (because it imports skilled labor).

Priority questions:
• Who is not currently being educated?
• How can community colleges help improve access to careers for underserved students while also serving the workforce needs of employers?
• How can we create a system where students can go back and forth between college and work and not get locked out or stuck on the lower rungs of the job ladder?

Florida

Storyline statement:
Community colleges can help to increase diversification of Florida's economy away from reliance on agriculture and tourism by helping attract high-wage, high-tech jobs.

Priority questions:
• Florida takes a "pipeline approach" to producing the skilled workforce needed to attract high-tech jobs. Where is the pipeline leaking? Where are we losing students, and what kind of students are we losing? How can we improve student progression within and across education levels?
• How does high school preparation affect postsecondary success, and how can the postsecondary readiness of K–12 students be enhanced?

Washington State

Storyline statement:
Community colleges are about creating opportunities, particularly for low-income populations.

Priority questions:
• Who are the students who are dropping out before they make it to the "tipping point" (at least a year of college and an occupational credential)?
• Why are they dropping out, and what can be done to improve their retention?
• How can students be encouraged to pursue education beyond the tipping point?

Lesson Two. States are most likely to stimulate systemic and sustainable reform when data are used to inform and empower educators.

SUR data collected at the state level are most useful for identifying "leakage points" in the educational pipeline and motivating action to address them. SUR data are not so useful in diagnosing the causes of leaks or other problems with student achievement, or in determining exactly what should be done to address them. Diagnosis of achievement gaps and development of strategies for improving outcomes should be left to those best positioned and equipped to do so: faculty, student services staff, and administrators. Therefore, whenever possible, states should disaggregate state-level analyses by college and make the results available to colleges for their own use.

States should also support efforts by colleges to review the results of research on student outcomes and devise strategies for improving student outcomes. Faculty and other college personnel should be allowed to analyze and discuss data on gaps in student achievement without concern that the information will be used to evaluate their individual performance or that of their institution. This will increase buy-in from practitioners for the solutions generated through the process and increase the chances that they will be implemented on a substantial scale.

Besides identifying problems, SUR data are also useful in measuring the impact of policies and practices designed to address problems in student achievement. For example, the Washington State Board of Community and Technical College System I-BEST program was designed to determine the tipping point at which credits and credentials begin to pay off in the workplace. Similarly, the Florida Community College System recently used unit record data to demonstrate the effectiveness of "college success" courses in increasing the rate at which students complete credentials or transfer (Windham, 2006; Zeidenberg, Jenkins, and Calcagno, 2007). This finding has spurred some colleges to require a student success course, particularly for students needing remedial instruction.

Lesson Three. Benchmarking performance across states can motivate efforts to improve student success and focus policy maker attention. The *Measuring Up* report cards have shown the value of having comparable performance data on higher education systems across states.

The community college state system directors involved with the State Data and Community College Student Success Project are keenly interested in working together to develop performance measures that can be compared across states. The reason, they say, is that policy makers frequently ask them how the performance statistics they report on their own colleges and systems compare with those from other states. Only with comparable measures will they be able answer the question, How well are we doing compared to other states? With the Measuring Up indicators, state officials can use information about the relative performance of their community colleges compared with that of other states to highlight areas for improvement and rally colleges to tackle them.

On the basis of his analysis of SUR data on community college students collected by the eleven states, Ewell (2006) concluded that most of these states currently have the data to generate a core set of common performance measures that could be compared across states. Measures like these are best used as dashboard indicators of the overall performance of states, or colleges within them. That is, they can help state systems and individual community colleges identify where problems are present and therefore the places where they should dig deeper.

Lesson Four. Effectively communicating findings and implications of research using SUR data is essential for persuading college leaders, policy makers, and other stakeholders to act. In communicating the results of research to policy makers and other stakeholders, it is important to develop a compelling message that can be delivered clearly and concisely. According to Earl Hale, former executive director of the Washington State Community and Technical College Board, "you have to speak plain English and do it in seven seconds" (E. Hale, personal communication, 2006). The tipping point identified by the Washington State Board for Community and Technical Colleges as the minimum amount of postsecondary education needed to secure a job paying family-supporting wages (Prince and Jenkins, 2005) is a good example of a succinct concept that has helped to change the policy discussion about education for low-skill adults in that state.

At the same time, it is important to present enough explanation of research findings so that policy makers and other audiences can accurately interpret the information being presented. For example, data on racial gaps in student attainment might reinforce stereotypes among some audiences that students from these groups are inherently deficient in abilities and attitudes, unless such data are accompanied by an explanation of the underlying factors. Clear and concise graphics can be useful in communicating complex information effectively.

Barriers to Using SUR Data for Improvement

The site visits to these eleven states also uncovered a range of barriers to using SUR data effectively as well as some effective practices for overcoming these barriers.

Barrier One. Policy makers are often unaware of the potential of SUR data for informing improvements in student outcomes; hence, they underinvest in state data and research capacity. Community college state agency research staffs are generally spread thin, which limits their capacity to analyze data collected at the state level. Often, they cannot do much more than the data analysis and reporting required for statutory compliance. Furthermore, because few policy makers understand the importance of analysis, they are also frequently cut when funding is tight.

The NCHEMS-led teams found only two states (Florida and Washington) among the eleven they visited that indicated they have enough staffing and resources to do research for improvement. Both states have been effective in securing funding to hire research staff because of the widespread visibility and policy impact of the studies they have conducted. For example, the Washington State Board for Community and Technical Colleges recently approved the hiring of another staff researcher in large part because of its success in using research to secure funding from the legislature. Florida has had a similar experience in building a stakeholder constituency for policy research based on longitudinal data-particularly in such areas as linking early success in gatekeeper courses with having taken rigorous courses in high school.

Barrier Two. Limitations imposed by laws and concerns about information privacy and security can make it difficult to share data across educational systems and between state agencies and institutions.

The Family Educational Rights and Privacy Act (FERPA) primarily governs privacy policies regarding the sharing of educational record data. The act applies to all educational institutions that receive federal funds; the secretary of education is empowered to withhold such funds if an institution is deemed not to be in compliance. Basically, FERPA gives parents and eligible students the right to inspect educational records maintained by schools, and the right to request that a school correct records believed to be in error. Recognizing the need to share such information under certain circumstances, FERPA allows institutions to disclose student-record information without consent for a variety of reasons, notably to improve instruction so long as the research is conducted in a manner that does not permit identification of individual subjects.

Though apparently straightforward, FERPA provisions have been interpreted in many ways when applied to the matter of matching student records electronically. More particularly, state-level interpretations of how to handle privacy rights for student records vary substantially. In most cases, FERPA is not seen as standing in the way of limited record matching for purposes of conducting student retention and completion studies within a state. But to avoid problems with FERPA, states and community college systems must make a clear case that the information resulting from any match will be useful for improving instruction and policies related to instruction. States should also establish clear, written ground rules that govern who can have access to SUR data and for what purposes. The Data Quality Campaign (Winnick, Palmer, and Coleman, 2006) has prepared a useful layman's guide to FERPA. A similarly useful publication on this topic has been prepared by Jobs for the Future (Mills, 2005).

Because of FERPA restrictions, states are limited in their ability to offer colleges unit record data on their students that have been matched with data from other sources and that still have personal identifiers such as social security numbers. For example, none of the eleven states included in the NCHEMS audit supplies individual colleges with unit record data on transfers to baccalaureate institutions. Some of these states do furnish aggregate information on the transfer rate and the success of transfer students. But without the unit record data, community colleges are not able to examine the relation between students' course-taking behavior and their use of services at their institution on the one hand and transfer to and performance at four-year institutions on the other hand. This sort of information would be useful to colleges in identifying barriers to transfer and evaluating the success of efforts to improve transfer outcomes.

Barrier Three. Initial demand for research based on SUR data is usually not strong from colleges, which, like states, generally use the data they collect for compliance rather than improvement.

A recent national study of community college institutional research offices found that very few colleges do more data analysis than is required for compliance reporting and accreditation (Morest and Jenkins, 2007). This is the case even though most colleges collect data that could be used to inform improvements in programs and services. One reason is limited capacity: more than half of community colleges employ no more than one full-time IR staff person. The study also revealed strong skepticism among community college administrators and faculty that the sort of data colleges report to states and the federal government for accountability purposes is useful for informing improvements in practice that could benefit students. Indeed, many colleges contend that the effort needed to produce compliance reports saps resources and energy from institutional research projects they believe would help to guide changes in practice that lead to improved student outcomes. Even where one finds willingness and resources to use data and research to improve programs and services, there is often little knowledge about how to do so.

Suggestions for Strengthening State Use of SUR Data for Improvement

From the experience of states that have had success using SUR data to inform improvements in policy and practice, we make a number of suggestions to other states seeking to strengthen their capacity to do the same.

- Identify your strategic goals for student performance improvement, and encapsulate them in a storyline that succinctly conveys what you are trying to accomplish and why.
- Review your performance indicators, and if necessary revise them to ensure that they are aligned with your strategic goals.
- Identify research questions that if answered could help advance your strategic goals; involve key stakeholders such as college personnel, other state agency staff, and governor's or legislative staff in defining and helping to prioritize the research questions.
- Conduct research on priority questions using data available at the state level; where feasible, disaggregate the results by college.

- Engage stakeholders at the state and college levels in interpreting the findings and considering the implications for policy and practice; encourage colleges to conduct further research to diagnose the causes of the gaps in student achievement identified, and formulate solutions based on that diagnosis.
- Work with stakeholders to develop a communications strategy with a compelling message consistent with the research findings that will motivate and guide action on policy and practice.
- Use SUR data to evaluate the effectiveness and impacts of efforts to improve outcomes for students.

Most policy makers are especially interested in the connection between education and jobs. Do students get jobs? What is the impact of their education on earnings? Are we training enough workers in the right fields? Therefore, we strongly urge states to develop SUR databases that allow tracking of students across levels of education and into the labor market. This requires states to match SUR education data with unemployment insurance wage records collected by state employment offices. Tracking students across levels of education and into the labor market makes it possible to show policy makers what the pipeline for their state's skilled workforce looks like and where there are leaks in the pipeline that need to be addressed.

Our discussion of barriers to using SUR for improvement indicates that it is often necessary to build a constituency for improvement-oriented research among college leaders and state policy makers. States can begin to demonstrate the power of SUR analysis to inform and evaluate efforts to improve outcomes for students by following the guidelines above, starting with an issue of pressing interest—say, improving developmental education outcomes or increasing the rate of baccalaureate transfer. Publicizing the results of particularly striking or revealing studies in easily communicated, nontechnical ways can help build support for further investment in data collection and research.

The process of generating enthusiasm among policy makers and practitioners for research on SUR data can take a long time. The Florida Department of Education's Community College and Workforce Development Division and the Washington State Board for Community and Technical Colleges, two national leaders in this regard, have each spent a decade or more building awareness and support for their research efforts. Thanks to their persistence, both states have reached the point where college leaders and policy makers not only welcome but expect research-based guidance from their state agencies on strategies for improving college and system performance. In these states and others, furnishing data to justify requests for funding and support strategic initiatives has helped make the community college agency much more effective with policy makers. Their practice of evaluating the effects of changes in policy and practice also signals to policy makers that community colleges in these states are willing to be held accountable for outcomes and are committed to improving performance over time. This increases the legitimacy of community colleges in the eyes of policy makers.

Research at the state level helps to leverage the efforts of individual colleges to conduct studies of student progression using college-level data. Both states and colleges are enlisting the support of university researchers, who are beginning to recognize the power of SUR data, to conduct systematic studies of student success and thus supplement their own often limited capacity for research.

In addition to working internally within their own states, state community college agencies can build support for using data and research for improvement by collaborating with other states to develop and pilot common performance indicators. As mentioned, this is one of the activities being undertaken by the states involved in the State Data and Community College Student Success Project. Regional educational entities such as the Southern Regional Education Board (SREB) have supported states in piloting measures for K–12 education; it is conceivable that they could be persuaded to do the same for community college measures. States can also support the Data Quality Campaign, a national collaborative effort to encourage state lawmakers to implement state SUR longitudinal tracking systems to improve student achievement.

In short, SUR data are a promising resource for states and community colleges to improve student success rates and help meet the workforce and civic needs of communities and regions. Although some progress has been made in tapping their potential, more systematic efforts taking advantage of what we know about what works in practice will help render these resources even more valuable.

References

Ewell, P. "Reaching Consensus on Common Indicators: A Feasibility Analysis." Paper prepared for the Achieving the Dream-Bridges to Opportunity State Data and Community College Student Success project meeting, San Antonio, Tex., January 2006.

Ewell, P., and Boeke, M. *Critical Connections: Linking States' Unit Record Systems to Track Student Progress.* Indianapolis, Ind.: Lumina Foundation for Education, 2007. http://www.luminafoundation.org/publications/Critical_Connections_Web.pdf (accessed May 31, 2008).

Mills, J. *State Data Systems and Privacy Concerns: Strategies for Balancing Public Interests.* Boston, Mass.: Jobs for the Future, 2005. http://www.jff.org/Documents/StateData-Systems.pdf (accessed May 31, 2008).

Morest, V. S., and Jenkins, D. *Institutional Research and the Culture of Evidence at Community Colleges.* New York: Community College Research Center, Teachers College, Columbia University, 2007.

Prince, D., and Jenkins, D. *Building Pathways to Success for Low-Skill Adults: Lessons for Community College Policy and Practice from a Statewide Longitudinal Tracking Study.* New York: Community College Research Center, Teachers College, Columbia University, 2005.

Windham, P. *Taking Student Life Skills Course Increases Student Success.* Tallahassee: Florida Community College System, 2006.

Winnick, S. Y., Palmer, S. R., and Coleman, A. L. *State Longitudinal Data Systems and Student Privacy Protections Under the Family Education Rights and Privacy Act.* Washington, D.C.: Holland and Knight, 2006.

Zeidenberg, M., Jenkins, D., and Calcagno, J. C. *Do Student Success Courses Actually Help Community College Students Succeed?* CCRC Brief No. 36. New York: Community College Research Center, Teachers College, Columbia University, 2007.

PETER EWELL is vice president of the National Center for Higher Education Management Systems.

DAVIS JENKINS is senior research associate at the Community College Research Center at Teachers College, Columbia University.

NEW DIRECTIONS FOR COMMUNITY COLLEGES • DOI: 10.1002/cc

8

This chapter introduces four new data tools that broaden student tracking coverage and add statistical indicators and visual images of employment patterns.

Beyond Higher Education: Other Sources of Data for Tracking Students

David Stevens

This chapter covers four extensions of postsecondary student tracking capability: a convenient way to record a current or former student's status as a federal employee, and three new Census Bureau tools that deliver user-defined insights about geographic, demographic, and economic target markets.

Tracking a student beyond postsecondary education can mean looking forward or backward in time, each being important for certain decision-making applications. Forward tracking of former students into employment affiliation helps answer an accountability question: What work-based return on the investment have our former students experienced? Backward tracking of current and former students is more novel. It can offer a response to another strategic planning question: Can awareness of the past work history of students help us align curriculum content to what current and future enrollees will need if they are to enter, and advance in, tomorrow's workforce?

The four data tools covered in this chapter deliver complementary types of information about the role of postsecondary education in labor markets—achieved and potential. A frontier of opportunity is opened, adding value to the student tracking capability that until now has typically delivered only limited coverage of a departing student's employment history and affiliations. Few current tracking systems offer more than limited information about whether or not students were employed, their quarterly income, and classification of industries in which they were employed.

In this chapter, the Federal Employment Data Exchange System is first introduced, with examples of how the information can be used in both

performance accountability and strategic planning applications. Later sections offer a three-part treatment of new user-defined Census Bureau Longitudinal Employer-Household Dynamics (LEHD) analytical tools: Quarterly Workforce Indicators Online, an industry focus ranking tool; and a new geographic information system product called On the Map.

The Federal Employment Data Exchange System

This section begins with answers to two basic questions about current student tracking capabilities: Is federal government employment covered in state unemployment insurance (UI) wage records that many state student tracking systems use? Is current and projected federal government hiring important enough outside the immediate Washington, D.C., area to justify an extension of student tracking coverage to include federal employment affiliations?

The Coverage Gap and the Importance of Responding. Federal government civilian employees and military personnel are not included in state UI wage report files, an administrative data source typically relied on to document the initial and subsequent employment history of former students. This exclusion has a negative impact on the accuracy of both state and local postsecondary strategic planning and accountability initiatives.

Currently, 87 percent of federal civilian employees work beyond the Washington, D.C., metropolitan area (Office of Personnel Management, 2007). In those geographic areas with a large number of federal employees, the absence of data about them in UI wage records may well produce substantial undercounting of students who obtain and persist in employment or join the military after leaving the community college. For institutions or states that use postcollege employment or military service as a measure of institutional or program effectiveness, this situation can have adverse effects, especially if resource allocations are linked to effectiveness measures. Moreover, the federal Office of Personnel Management estimates that 60 percent of the federal workforce will be eligible to retire within the next ten years (U.S. Office of Personnel Management, 2007). The opportunity for postsecondary institutions to help refill the federal workforce pipeline will not be limited to a few mid-Atlantic states.

Since 2003, the Office of Performance and Technology in the Employment and Training Administration of the U.S. Department of Labor has supported a Federal Employment Data Exchange System (FEDES). Federal funding covering overall management of the system and processing of data-sharing agreements with states has been awarded to the Maryland Department of Labor, Licensing, and Regulation. This Maryland state agency has subcontracted management of the national data processing portal to the Jacob France Institute at the University of Baltimore. To date, states have not been required to pay for use of the system. FEDES serves as a convenient way for a postsecondary school or state higher education authority to record a current or former student's status as a federal government civilian employee, postal service worker, or active-duty member of the military.

An accurate student social security number is required to take advantage of FEDES. This does not mean that the social security number has to be the identifier that is used by a postsecondary institution or state education authority to achieve other internal and external data linkage goals; there just has to be a capability to accomplish a one-time link of the social security number with the other student identifier. The remainder of the time the social security number can be stored beyond the reach of unauthorized parties.

Access to status information about federal government civilian employees and postal service workers is authorized if the request contributes to a federal performance measurement initiative required by the U.S. Office of Management and Budget or federal law, or if the request contributes to a state performance measurement or reporting requirement authorized under state law or regulation. The transacting parties must approve in advance requests for access that do not satisfy any of these authorized use criteria. Current U.S. Department of Defense policy is more restrictive; it does not allow the release of active-duty military personnel information for a proposed use that is authorized only under state law or regulation.

Legal authority to participate in FEDES begins with negotiation and signing of a memorandum of understanding, or data-sharing agreement. The Maryland Department of Labor, Licensing, and Regulation and a single state agency, which is almost always the state agency that receives federal Workforce Investment Act funds, are the parties to this legal document. The phrase "almost always" can be important to state postsecondary education authorities and institutions. If the state agency that receives Workforce Investment Act funds chooses not to participate in the system, another state agency can do so.

The legal negotiation process begins with a uniform template, but differences in state laws and regulations are accommodated using modified language. An important end result of the legal negotiation process is that there is a legal authority in each participating state that accepts responsibility for satisfaction of defined time schedule, data processing, and security requirements set forth in the memorandum of understanding. As a practical matter, it is desirable to have a single point of contact in each state. However, exceptions have been recognized and accepted.

Interstate, and sometimes intrastate, differences surface in deciding under what conditions prior consent is not required to disclose information under the Family Educational Rights and Privacy Act. In general, an educational agency or institution can disclose personally identifiable information from an education record of a student without consent if the disclosure is to organizations conducting studies on behalf of educational agencies to improve instruction.

Beyond the federal statutory authority, some state education entities encounter state restrictions on sharing of student information with a noneducation entity, such as the state agency that receives federal Workforce Investment Act funds. In such cases, the Jacob France Institute has waived the state single point-of-contact requirement that is sought for efficient

NEW DIRECTIONS FOR COMMUNITY COLLEGES • DOI: 10.1002/cc

management of the overall data processing responsibility. Student record extract information is allowed to flow directly from a state education authority to the Jacob France Institute.

The Data Exchange Process Works. A quarterly data matching cycle begins when organizations within a state deliver their unit record files to the single designated state agency that will bundle these files for transmittal to the Jacob France Institute. If a waiver has been granted, the delivery of data occurs directly from an authorized organization to the institute. Once the stable quarterly schedule has been announced, the institute opens a secure, state-specific, password-protected repository for each participating state to upload its file of unit-record data. Each unit record must satisfy a uniform specification. Fields are defined for student social security number, year, quarter, state, within-state program, and a flag indicating whether an intended use satisfies the Department of Defense restrictive criteria.

After the deadline for acceptance of state unit-record extract files has passed, the institute creates a master file of social security numbers that have been received for processing in this cycle. This is why each unit-record extract includes data fields for state, program, and Department of Defense compliance; a student can appear more than once in a data processing cycle, within a state or in more than one state. The full master file of social security numbers is delivered to the federal Office of Personnel Management and to the U.S. Postal Service. A subfile of this master, containing only the complying use records, is delivered to the Department of Defense.

Again on a tight and predefined turnaround schedule, matched record extracts covering the most recent two years of available personnel information are returned by the Office of Personnel Management, U.S. Postal Service, and Department of Defense to the Jacob France Institute. These matched record extracts are then processed for secure uploading to be retrieved by states, once more on a predefined time schedule that does not permit files to languish online.

Standard matched record data fields returned to states by the Office of Personnel Management, U.S. Postal Service, and Department of Defense include dates that can be used to calculate employment start date and end date if applicable, and earnings amount for a defined time period. The Office of Personnel Management matched record extract file also contains fields for state, federal agency, and occupation; the U.S. Postal Service file includes fields for location of employment and job title, and the Department of Defense file includes fields for duty location and occupation. Historical coverage is limited to two years at the time of a particular query of federal employment records. Later queries submitted at a two-year interval can extend coverage for an unlimited time span.

One advantage of adding federal employment information to a student tracking system is that location, unit affiliation, and occupational classification can be monitored beyond the initial transition destination. This enables renewable feedback about the geographic, organizational, and occupational paths taken by former students. It also supports analysis of periodic reenrollment events and how they may influence or be influenced by career trajectories.

Each quarterly cycle of FEDES processing covers the most recent two years of personnel action information, with no more than a three-month lag from the actual data of a matching transaction. This means that timely action to include a file of newly enrolled students in a record matching cycle has the potential to return up to six quarters of pre-enrollment employment information. This in turn can support an automated student profiling exercise that does not depend on self-reported information that is subject to nonresponse and other data quality threats.

A neglected feature of the FEDES capability is that reported occupational classification information can be used to map the occupational experience of enrolled students as a potential instructional asset. Disclosure rules prohibit using a student's recent work history as a guide to ask for her help in design and delivery of a course module, but such information can be followed by e-circulation of a request for targeted assistance that is based on defined types of work experience.

New Census Bureau Tools

Up to this point, attention has focused on extended coverage of student employment affiliations. The focus turns next to the three new Census Bureau tools that deliver rich contextual information about the economies where students are expected to seek work once they leave a postsecondary institution.

Before proceeding, an explicit reminder is needed about how tracking students is defined in this chapter. A typical student tracking capability assigns a unique identifier to a person and follows this individual, recording predefined statuses through time. This chapter's extension of the traditional student tracking approach adds three Census Bureau tools that deliver routinely updated information about successful matches of workers and jobs—tracking hiring flows and job creation trends by location, industry, gender, and age group.

Quarterly Workforce Indicators Online. Multiple features of Quarterly Workforce Indicators Online are pioneering. Postsecondary institutional researchers can take advantage of these technical advances to improve the quality and relevance of information and analyses passed forward to decision makers.

A breakthrough statistical approach permits release of more detailed information than was possible under the Bureau of Labor Statistics standard for protection of business and worker identities, while still ensuring anonymity to both businesses and workers. Precedent-setting linkage of confidential data sources behind the Census Bureau firewall allows release of Quarterly Workforce Indicator online snapshots and trends by gender and age group, as well as by previously available industry and geographic descriptors.

NEW DIRECTIONS FOR COMMUNITY COLLEGES • DOI: 10.1002/cc

Quarterly Workforce Indicators Online delivers eight indicator series, including new hires, average new hire earnings, and job creation. Each indicator series is available by a choice of substate geographic classification, age group, gender, and North American Industry Classification System (NAICS) code. All are updated quarterly with a nine-month lag in online availability. For example, in July 2008 the most recent indicator data in most cases would be for the July–September 2007 quarter. Historical coverage since 2001 can be accessed online for all of the forty-four states that are current Census Bureau partners. Some states have as much as another decade of coverage. User-defined choices from the Quarterly Workforce Indicators Online Website are year, quarter, geographic area, industry code (or the sum of all industries), inclusion of private sector businesses, gender, and age group.

In a matter of a few minutes, a user can select, see, and print out an eight-by-four table containing thirty-two numbers: four columns defined by choice of geography and time, and eight Quarterly Workforce Indicator rows. Exhibit 8.1 presents output for a Workforce Investment Act region in northern Cook County, Illinois. A single additional click brings up a pivot table comparison opportunity. The user can then select a column (geography, industry, gender, age group, business ownership category, or year), a row (one of the Quarterly Workforce Indicators), and a year (from all years of data available for the designated state) and immediately see new results.

Exhibit 8.1. LEAD State of Illinois WIA Reports: Quarterly Workforce Indicators

Select criteria below. A new report will be created below as selections change.

Year [2006 ▼]   Geographic grouping [WIA ▼] **or Information by Detailed Industry** County | Metro | WIA or Detailed Industry

Quarter [Q3 ▼]   WIA [08 WB of Northern Cook County ▼]

Sex [Male and Female ▼]   Industry [All NAICS Sectors ▼]

Age group [14-99 ▼]   Ownership [All(1-5) ▼] [Generate Report]

QWI Quick Facts	WB of Northern Cook County (Q3)	WB of Northern Cook County (Avg.: Selected + 3 Prior Qtrs.)	Illinois (Q3)	Illinois (Avg.: Selected + 3 Prior Qtrs.)
① Total employment	654,845	647,391	5,757,932	5,680,192
② Net job flows	−11,447	2,600	−64,734	38,555
③ Job creation	23,006	30,247	225,916	284,556
④ New hires	98,665	92,084	943,732	845,338
⑤ Separations	124,885	108,320	1,143,084	990,131
⑥ Turnover	9.7%	9.4%	10.1%	9.7%
⑦ Avg. monthly earnings	$4,229.00	$4,430.50	$3,716.00	$3,833.75
⑧ Avg. new hire earnings	$2,513.00	$2,680.25	$2,265.00	$2,390.75

NEW DIRECTIONS FOR COMMUNITY COLLEGES • DOI: 10.1002/cc

Skepticism is sometimes expressed about the relevance of year-old data for forward-looking postsecondary education decision making. An accurate five-to–ten-year projection of anticipated business hiring needs is said to be required for decisions about capital investment priorities, faculty recruitment strategies, and curriculum designs. If so, informed strategic decision making will forever remain beyond our reach.

We cannot know whether a projection is accurate until after the defined end date has passed. Instead, we depend on a combination of carefully selected historical information and a practical mix of future trajectory guesses. The Quarterly Workforce Indicators Online capability is a remarkable new tool offering access to high-quality historical information in a convenient way that requires no unusual training or skills.

Examples of User-Defined Applications. If a demographic profile of recently enrolled students is available, the user-controlled selections of age group, gender, and geographic area can be used to align indicator values with this profile. Insight is thereby gained about where (geographically and by industry sector) job creation and hiring action has occurred for demographics such as this student population. If state UI wage record tracking has been used, this portrait of overall hiring activity can be compared to the known employment destinations of a defined cohort of former students.

New awareness of Quarterly Workforce Indicators Online data can trigger a series of locally initiated inquiries posed to the business community. The Quarterly Workforce Indicators product does not currently include educational attainment or occupation as user-defined selection tools. Having accomplished high value-added through addition of previously unavailable age group and gender descriptors of new-hires activity, the capability stops short of the still unreachable goal of educational attainment and occupational specificity for new-hires activity.

Beginning with Quarterly Workforce Indicators Online evidence about where recent hiring activity has been concentrated for defined age-gender subpopulations that align with student demographics, targeted inquiries can be made to business representatives who are responsible for hiring, asking which occupations make up the flow of hires and what educational attainment is expected for successful candidacy. Answers can be assembled into diverse formats for delivery to institutional leaders, current students, and through various media channels to potential future students.

The User-Defined Industry Focus Tool. The Industry Focus tool draws on the same base data files as Quarterly Workforce Indicators Online, but it offers other user-defined ways to recover and display indicator information. It adds four new user-defining opportunities: the number of industries to be ranked and displayed, whether or not to include a particular industry, which of the eight Quarterly Workforce Indicators to use as the ranking criterion, and which one or more of the indicator values to display. Time coverage is predefined as the most recent four quarters available for the state in question. Each of the user-defined indicator values displayed is a four-quarter average based on the predefined time coverage.

Industry Focus does what the title implies: it anticipates that many users will seek laserlike targeting of the most promising industries only, where promise is user-defined. It may be the highest ranking of new hires for a designated combination of age group and gender, or the highest ranking of average monthly earnings for new hires, or another of the eight indicator options to choose among. Exhibit 8.2 shows the list of variables upon which results can be ranked.

Two cautions about use of the Industry Focus tool should be heeded. First, the Industry Focus indicator titled number of new hires includes only new-hire transactions that result in sustained affiliation with the same employer over three consecutive quarters. This is a subset of the larger Quarterly Workforce Indicators Online New Hires indicator that includes all new employees in a reference year or quarter except recalls of former employees who had worked for this employer at any time during the previous three quarters. The second caution is that average monthly earnings for new hires includes all levels of educational attainment and all types of previous work history, both unobserved. This caution is of particular importance to postsecondary educators because they will not be able to determine earnings for employees who attain a stipulated level of education or degree. For example, combining data for employees who have only a high school education up through a graduate degree will not help a community college assess earnings for associate degree recipients or those with some college.

On the Map

On the Map is the last of the four new data tools covered in this chapter; it is saved for last because it combines user-defined geographic information system maps with statistical reports based on the same database as the Quarterly Workforce Indicators Online and Industry focus tools. On the Map is under continuous refinement, and a new version is scheduled for release in September 2008.

Users of the On the Map online software can select from predefined geographic areas identical to the Quarterly Workforce Indicators Online and

Exhibit 8.2. List of Variables

⊙ ☑ Employment ⓐ
○ ☐ Growth in employment ⓐ
○ ☐ Growth in hiring ⓐ
○ ☐ Number of new hires ⓐ
○ ☐ Firm job change ⓐ
○ ☐ Average monthly earnings for all workers ⓐ
○ ☐ Growth in average monthly earnings for all workers ⓐ
○ ☐ Average monthly earnings for new hires ⓐ

Industry Focus geographic options, or a user can draw a geographic boundary of interest. Then the user can choose between a map that displays where residents in this area work (labeled a commute shed) or where people who work in this area live (labeled a labor shed).

A concentric circles mapping feature allows users to select from predefined circle diameters that display geographic concentrations of worker residences and workplaces. This should be of particular interest to postsecondary institutions that do not have well-defined perimeters of student attraction or business recruitment.

A buffered selection tool allows a user to choose a particular highway corridor paired with a choice of commute shed or labor shed mapping display and production of associated statistical reports. Again, this feature of On the Map anticipates what users such as institutional researchers affiliated with postsecondary education institutions will want to see.

Currently, the On the Map database is updated annually, with more than a one-year lag in coverage. Protection of individual and business anonymity has been given a high priority in designing the online interactive On the Map software. A new user should not expect to see on her or his computer monitor, or be able to download in a statistical report, the identity of a business enterprise or residential location. Instead, On the Map has been designed to deliver visual and statistical profiles of where people live and work. Then, within a user-defined area, the online Quarterly Workforce Indicators Online and Industry Focus tools can be used to learn more about the demographics and industry mix within the area.

Marketing Uses of an Extended Student Tracking Capacity

The Federal Employment Data Exchange System offers state postsecondary systems and institutions a convenient way to improve awareness of student federal civilian employee agency affiliations and occupations before, concurrent with, and following enrollment. Similar time coverage of active-duty military service information may also be available, contingent on satisfaction of the established criteria for authorized use.

A federal employment database assembled over time can be used to design and release focused briefs targeting specific constituencies. Student recruitment efforts can incorporate reliable information about when and how other federal employees have taken advantage of postsecondary opportunities and with what subsequent impact on their career. Institutional leadership teams can be alerted to recent changes in the number and mix of agencies and occupations of federal civilian employees who enroll. Program managers and instructional staff members within an institution can be given feedback about recent changes in federal government agency and occupational destinations of departing students. Currently enrolled students who will soon leave can be informed about recent federal government employment transition paths taken by predecessors. Again, a valid student social security number is required to begin the FEDES process. Everyone has Web access to the Census Bureau Quarterly Workforce Indicators Online, Industry Focus, and On the Map tools.

Each of the three Census Bureau Web tools covered in this chapter can be used alone or with one or both of the other tools. Web-based guides to proper use are available. One-time investment in learning about the full potential of each tool will open the door to a broad portfolio of new user-defined analytical opportunities.

A postsecondary institutional researcher can begin with On the Map, locate her own institution first, and then select among concentric circle, corridor, or freehand-drawn boundaries to acquire a basic familiarity with relevant concentrations of workplaces and worker residences. Statistical reports downloaded from the On the Map site will point the way to focused use of the Industry Focus and Quarterly Workforce Indicators Online tools, each offering more extensive historical time coverage and user-defined opportunities to explore seasonal and cyclical sensitivity of hiring and job creation flows.

A metaphor conveys how the new Census Bureau tools extend an institutional researcher's analytical vision. We have all seen after-dark satellite images that reveal only concentrated clusters of lighted buildings and infrastructure. Think of these clusters of light as the limited information that is available from traditional student tracking systems, each former student being a light source. Substitute a daylight satellite image of the same area, and many other features are now visible. This is what the Census Bureau tools add: contextual features of the "black box" that former students enter in traditional limited student tracking systems.

Conclusion

This chapter has introduced new tools that broaden and deepen student tracking system capabilities. Proper use of each tool requires an initial investment of time to become comfortable with and take full advantage of user-defined options. The tools are so new that refinements should be expected.

Reference

U.S. Office of Personnel Management. *2006 Performance and Accountability Report*. Washington, D.C.: U.S. Office of Personnel Management, 2007. http://www.opm.gov/gpra/opmgpra/par2006/ (accessed May 31, 2008).

DAVID STEVENS *is executive director of the Jacob France Institute and professor of economics at the University of Baltimore.*

This brief concluding chapter offers final observations and potential new developments in tracking community college students.

Conclusion and the Future

Trudy H. Bers

This *New Directions* was not planned as an issue on student unit records. But as each chapter arrived, it became clear to me that accurately tracking students and using resulting data to understand student behavior, attendance patterns, and success by almost any definition other than self-reported "I was successful" assertions must rest on examining student unit records. A decade ago, universities might have supplied feeder community colleges with aggregated data depicting the academic achievements of all transfers from the college, and that would have been deemed adequate, if not terribly useful, information. This is no longer the case.

Long used within an institution, often on a term-by-term basis, student information management systems (SIMS) application, placement, course registration, financial aid, grade, and graduation records yield information about what students actually do and achieve within a college or university. Less commonly, especially in community colleges, are these records linked with results from surveys such as the Community College Survey of Student Engagement, the Noel-Levitz Satisfaction Survey, or even institutionally developed instruments. Community colleges rarely connect a student's SIMS records with data about the student's participation in co- and extracurricular activities, on-campus employment, learning outcomes assessments, or other indicators of involvement and achievement. Additionally, building cohort longitudinal datasets that permit examining students' progress through an institution, not just performance within a given term, is a relatively new endeavor at many community colleges. For example, the requirement that institutions participating in Achieving the Dream use longitudinal

NEW DIRECTIONS FOR COMMUNITY COLLEGES, no. 143, Fall 2008 © 2008 Wiley Periodicals, Inc.
Published online in Wiley InterScience (www.interscience.wiley.com) • DOI: 10.1002/cc.339

data to measure student success marked the first venture into employing longitudinal data for many of these schools.

As demands for more data about student enrollments and achievements grow, so too is there growth in the construction and use of student unit record systems across sectors: K–12 and postsecondary education, the labor market, and other agencies such as the military and penal systems. Many chapters in this issue illustrate the complexities and benefits of pan-agency databases.

As I think about student tracking at the end of 2007, these observations seem especially germane. A shift in focus from access alone to access and success is a powerful driver behind tracking students and building datasets that permit this. For community colleges, successful transfer and success in the workplace are key indicators of institutional effectiveness, and they cannot be accurately measured in the absence of tracking students at the individual level. At least forty states have student tracking systems in place, although many include, primarily if not exclusively, data from public institutions only.

Nationally, we are beginning to recognize the numerous ways in which students move through the educational pipeline. They attend multiple institutions, often in patterns that conflict with traditional assumptions that students attend a community college and then transfer to a four-year college or university for a bachelor's degree. Instead, students enroll in multiple institutions at the same time, move from a baccalaureate institution to a community college, transfer between community colleges, earn college credit while in high school (witness the large increase in dual credit courses through which students earn both secondary and postsecondary credit), earn credit through documenting learning experiences, and more. Tracking students permits us to understand their behavior, and eventually to revise policies to more appropriately accommodate and support students whose attendance patterns do not conform to traditional assumptions such as enrollment in only one school at a time and transfer being in a linear fashion from the two-year to the four-year institution.

Because transfer is now recognized as an important indicator of success both for the individual student who transfers and for the community college whose students transfer, being able to document not just enrollment but also accumulation of credits and earning of degrees has grown in importance. In assessing student transfer, institutions use a variety of ways to identify students who transfer in, among them looking at the last school they attended or the school from which they received the most credits. Neither approach identifies all the institutions a student has attended; here, too, matching student unit records permits an institution to recognize all schools a student previously attended and give those schools feedback on all their students, not just those who meet a more limited definition of "transfer."

The Family Education Rights and Privacy Act (FERPA), mentioned by several chapter authors, affects the willingness of institutions to exchange student unit records. There is no single interpretation of FERPA. State attorneys general have offered differing perspectives on what FERPA does or does not allow, and legal counsels across institutions also differ in their advice. This creates a situation where some schools are more willing to share student unit record information than others. In addition to the patchwork of FERPA interpretations, a related impediment is what appears to be a growing reluctance of students to report social security numbers. This may be especially problematic in community colleges, where relatively few students apply for financial aid or work as student employees. Virtually all schools issue a unique student ID to be used internally, but absent a common unique identifier the accuracy with which records from disparate datasets can be linked is compromised.

Where do we stand with respect to federal policies regarding development of a national or federal student unit record system? Early on, the secretary's Commission on the Future of Higher Education, more popularly known as the Spellings Commission, seemed favorably inclined toward creation of such a system. However, the commission backed away from recommending such a system. In considering the reauthorization of the Higher Education Act, the U.S. Senate forbade creation of a national student unit record system. Reauthorization of the act had not occurred as of the end of 2007, so changes in relation to student unit records could still be incorporated in the final legislation.

Interest in pursuing such a system varies, for a number of reasons. A national system could be similar to but not the same as existing state systems, leading to cost and confusion. State sharing of data is already taking place, but the exponential complications that would ensue if each state had an agreement with every other state to exchange data would be huge. Put simply, if each state had an agreement with every other state, there would need to be 1,225 separate agreements. Interpretations of FERPA would further complicate the effort.

The American Association for Community Colleges (AACC) sees potential in a national student unit record system but is sensitive to the investment states have already made in creating their own systems and the burden that double reporting (state and federal) could impose on colleges. The AACC is also concerned about federally mandated success measures that are not appropriate for community colleges. Further, the association would want to be sure that colleges could get back their unit record information for use in institutional improvement.

As chapters in this New Directions make clear, a great deal of work and research is already taking place with respect to tracking community college students. This issue is certainly not exhaustive in its coverage of existing tracking initiatives, but it gives ample evidence that interest, creativity, good research, and sound use of results characterize student tracking projects at both the institutional and the state levels.

TRUDY H. BERS is executive director of research, curriculum, and planning at Oakton Community College.

INDEX

AACC. *See* American Association for Community Colleges (AACC)

AASCU. See American Association of State Colleges and Universities (AASCU)

ABE. *See* Adult basic education (ABE)

Achieving the Dream: Community Colleges Count, 2, 44, 72, 93–94

ACT testing, 38, 42

Adelman, C., 8

Adult basic education (ABE), 4, 60, 62–64, 67, 68

African Americans, 34, 61, 67

Agency for Workforce Innovation (Florida), 38, 41

American Association for Community Colleges (AACC), 95

American Association of State Colleges and Universities (AASCU), 51

Asians, 61

Associate in science programs, increasing completion rates in, 35–36

Bailey, A., 61

Bailey, T., 8, 59, 63

Bashford, J., 3, 31

Bers, T., 37, 93

Bloomer, T., 65

Boeke, M., 71

Borglum, K., 8

Building Pathways to Success for Low-Skill Adult Students: Lessons for Community College Policy and Practice from a Statewide Longitudinal Tracking Study (Prince and Jenkins), 62

Burd, S., 8

Bureau of Labor Statistics. *See* U.S. Bureau of Labor Statistics

Calcagno, J. C., 8, 59, 74

Carnevale, A. P., 60

CCR. *See* Course completion ratio (CCR)

Census Bureau. *See* U.S. Census Bureau

Certificate and degree completion file, 22

Coleman, A. L., 77

College Board, 38

College Placement Test, 42

Colorado, 72, 75

Commission on the Future of Higher Education (U.S. Department of Education), 42, 95. *See also* Spellings Commission

Community College and Workforce Development Division (Florida Department of Education), 79

Community College Bridges to Opportunity, 72

Community College Research Center, 66–67, 72

Community College Survey of Student Engagement, 15, 93

Connecticut, 72

Cook County, Illinois, 88

Course completion ratio (CCR), 10–11; SPSS file with, 11

Course schedule file, 21–22

Crosta, P., 8, 59, 67

Data Quality Campaign, 77, 80

Desrochers, D. M., 60

Developmental climb, 11–12; logic and step of, 13

Dillon, P., 8

Elliott, B., 61

English as a second language (ESL), 4, 60, 62–65, 67, 68

Enrollment file, 9–10; sample, in SPSS, 10

ESL. *See* English as a second language (ESL)

Ewell, P., 4, 71, 72, 76

External transfer data file, 22

FAFSA. See Federal application for financial aid (FAFSA)

Family Educational Rights and Privacy Act (FERPA), 25, 46, 47–49, 77, 85, 94–95

FCCS. *See* Florida: Community College System

Federal application for financial aid (FAFSA), 66

Federal Employment Data Exchange System (FEDES), 4, 38, 84–87, 91, 92;

coverage gap and importance of responding in, 84–86; efficacy of, 86–87; and marketing uses of extended student tracking capacity, 91–92

FEDES. *See* Federal Employment Data Exchange System (FEDES)

FERPA. *See* Family Educational Rights and Privacy Act (FERPA)

FETPIP. *See* Florida Education and Training Placement Information Program (FETPIP)

Florida, 3, 8, 31, 33, 72, 75, 77; Agency for Workforce Innovation, 38, 41; Board of Governors, 38; as case study for statewide student unit record system, 37–46; College Placement Test, 38; Community College System (FCCS), 43, 74; Comprehensive Assessment Tests, 38; Department of Children and Families, 38, 41; Department of Corrections, 38; Department of Education, 31, 38, 43; Department of Juvenile Justice, 38; Division of Accountability, Research, and Measurement (Department of Education), 48; Division of Community Colleges, 43; Education and Training Placement Information Program (FETPIP), 37–39, 41; Go Higher, Florida! task force, 42; Higher Education Funding Advisory Committee, 41; Independent Colleges and Universities of Florida, 38; K–20 accountability program, 42; K–20 Education Data Warehouse (EDW), 39, 41, 42; Postsecondary Education Access Task Force (ATF), 41; State Board of Education, 42; State University System (SUS), 43; Student Data Base (SDB), 43, 44; Student Data Course File (SDCF; State University System), 43, 44; Workforce Estimating Conference, 40

Florida Education and Training Placement Information Program (FETPIP), 37–39, 41

Ford Foundation, 72

Gardner, E., 60

GED, 23, 39, 41, 62–64

Go Higher, Florida! task force, 42

Graduation Rate Survey (GRS; Integrated Postsecondary Education Data System), 19, 23, 44–45

GRS. *See* Graduation Rate Survey (GRS; Integrated Postsecondary Education Data System)

Grubb, W. N., 63

Hagedorn, L. S., 3, 7, 8, 11, 15

Hale, E., 76

Higher Education Act, 95

Hispanics, 34, 61, 64, 67

I-Best program. See Integrated Basic Education and Skills Training (I-Best) program

Independent Colleges and Universities of Florida, 38

Industry Focus tool (U.S. Census Bureau), 89–92

Integrated Basic Education and Skills Training (I-Best) program, 4, 65, 66, 74

Integrated Postsecondary Education Data System (IPEDS), 19, 23, 25, 47, 49–51; Graduation Rate Survey (GRS), 19, 23, 25, 44–45; unique identifier (UNITID), 49

IPEDS. *See* Integrated Postsecondary Education Data System (IPEDS)

Jacob France Institute (University of Baltimore), 84–86

JCAR. *See* Joint Commission on Accountability Reporting (JCAR)

Jenkins, D., 4, 8, 59, 62, 65, 71, 74, 76, 77

Jobs for the Future, 72, 77

Joint Commission on Accountability Reporting (JCAR), 51

Jones, D., 59

Kentucky, 72

Kienzl, G. S., 63

Kress, A. M., 3, 7

Kubala, T., 8

Lasater, B., 61

Latinos, 61

Leinbach, T., 62

Lillibridge, F., 3, 19

Longitudinal Employer-Household Dynamics (LEHD) analytical tool (U.S. Census Bureau), 84

Longitudinal tracking: of low-skill adult students, 59–68; and statewide stu-

dent unit record system, 37–46; of student persistence and completion rate, 51–52
Los Angeles Community College District, 9
Louisiana, 72
Low-skill adult students: and changing economy, changing demographics, 60–61; education attainment and earnings for, 61–63; and reaching tipping point, 63–64; and student socioeconomic status, 66–67; using research to guide policy and practice for longitudinal tracking of, 59–68; and using study findings as catalyst for change, 64–66
Lucas, J. A., 8
Lumina Foundation for Education, 72

Marcotte, D. E., 63
Maryland Department of Labor, Licensing, and Regulation, 84, 85
Mathematics, increasing student success in, 32–33
Maxwell, W. E., 15
McGuinness, A., Jr., 59
MDC. See Miami Dade College (MDC)
Measuring Up, 74–76
Miami Dade College (MDC), 3, 31–36; Office of Institutional Research, 35; Quality Enhancement Plan (QEP), 33
Microsoft Access, 21
Microsoft Excel, 21
Microsoft PowerPoint, 28
Mills, J., 77
Mingle, J., 61
Minnesota, 4; Office of Higher Education, 50; State Colleges and Universities system, 49–51, 53, 54, 56
Moon, H. S., 15
Morest, V. S., 77
Mott, J., 8

National Center for Education Statistics (NCES), 1
National Center for Higher Education Management Systems (NCHEMS), 72, 77
National Governor's Association, 42
National Student Clearinghouse (NSC), 1–4, 25, 38, 43, 47–56; DegreeVerify service, 55, 56; StudentTracker service, 4, 48–51

Native Americans, 61, 67
NCES. See National Center for Education Statistics
NCHEMS. See National Center for Higher Education Management Systems (NCHEMS)
New Mexico, 72
Noel-Levitz Satisfaction Survey, 93
North American Industry Classification System (NAICS), 4, 88
North Carolina, 72
North Dakota, 50
NSC. See National Student Clearinghouse (NSC)
NSC StudentTracker, 4, 48–49; analysis and impact of data from, 53–54; completeness of, 53–54; improving student transfer tracking with, 54–55; legal framework used for, 56; limitations of, 55–56; and student persistence and completion rate, 51–52; uses of, 50–51; uses of persistence and completion measure in, 54

Office of Performance and Technology in the Employment and Training Administration (U.S. Department of Labor), 84
Office of Postsecondary Education ID number (OPEID), 49
Ohio, 72
On the Map tool (U.S. Census Bureau), 5, 90–92
OPEID. See Office of Postsecondary Education ID number (OPEID)

Palmer, S. R., 77
Patthey-Chavez, G. G., 8
Pell grants, 44
Pfeiffer, J., 3, 37
Prince, D., 4, 62, 65, 66, 76

Quarterly Workforce Indicators Online (U.S. Census Bureau), 4, 87–90, 92; New Hires indicator, 90

Reeves, R., 3–4, 47
Romano, R. M., 53
Rooker, L. S., 48

San Antonio, Texas, 72
SAS software, 21, 23, 28, 49
SAT testing, 42

Schoenecker, C., 3–4, 47

SDB. *See* Florida: Student Data Base

SDCF. *See* Florida: Student Data Course File

Semester Course File, 21, 23

Seppanen, L., 63

SES. *See* Socioeconomic status (SES)

SLS. *See* Student Life Skills (SLS) courses

Socioeconomic status (SES), 66–67

Socioeconomic Well-Being of Washington State: Who Attends Community and Technical Colleges (Prince), 66

South Dakota, 50

Southern Regional Education Board (SREB), 80

Spaulding, R., 63

Spellings Commission, 42, 95. *See also* Commission on the Future of Higher Education (U.S. Department of Education)

Spence, C., 65

SPSS software, 10, 11, 21, 28, 49, 51

State Data and Community College Student Success Project, 72, 74, 75, 80; sample strategic storylines and associated research from states involved in, 75

State unemployment insurance (UI) wage records, 84, 89

State University of New York, 53

Statewide student unit record system, 37–46

Stevens, D., 4, 83

Student Demographic File, 21, 22

Student Life Skills (SLS) courses, 31, 32, 34, 35, 44; examining impact of, 34–35

Student Right-to-Know and Campus Security Act of 1990, 19

Student tracking data: and examining five-year success rates by initial placement status and ethnicity, 33–34; and examining impact of student life skills courses, 34–35; and improving student success in mathematics, 32–33; and increasing completion rate in associate in science programs, 35–36; use of, from institutional perspective, 31–36

Student tracking model: analyzing data for, 26–28; and data files, 21–22; and determining student outcomes for each semester, 23–26; establishing cohort for, 22–23; evolution of, 29–30; and showing results, 28–29;

and starting with data, 20–21; using institutional data, 19–30; and using spreadsheet to calculate total completers, 28

Student unit record (SUR) data: barriers to using, 76–78; lessons from states that use, for improvement, 73–76; suggestions for strengthening use of, 78–80; using, to increase community college student success, 71–80

SUR data. *See* Student unit record (SUR) data

SUS. *See* Florida State University System

Texas, 72

Thomas-Spiegel, J., 8

Tinto, V., 15

Title IV, 19

Transcript analysis, 9–12; additional uses of, 12–15; and course completion ratio, 10–11; definition of, 7; and developmental climb, 11–12; and enrollment file, 9–10; overcoming limitations of, 15; and sample student transcript, 14 Table 1.2

Transfer and Retention of Urban Community College Students (TRUCCS) Project, 3, 9

TRUCCS. *See* Transfer and Retention of Urban Community College Students Project

UNITID (IPED unique identifier), 49

University of Baltimore, 84

University of California, Los Angeles, 9

University of Minnesota, 50

University of Southern California, 9

U.S. Bureau of Labor Statistics, 87

U.S. Census Bureau, 4, 83, 87–90; examples of user-defined applications, 89; Industry Focus tool, 89–90; Longitudinal Employer-Household Dynamics (LEHD) analytical tool, 84; On the Map, 90–91; Quarterly Workforce Indicators Online, 87–89

U.S. Department of Defense, 85, 86

U.S. Department of Education, 8, 37, 42; Commission on the Future of Higher Education, 42, 95; Spellings Commission, 42, 95

U.S. Department of Labor, 84; Office of Performance and Technology in Employment and Training Administration, 84

U.S. Office of Management and Budget, 85
U.S. Office of Personnel Management, 84, 86
U.S. Postal Service, 86
U.S. Senate, 95

Virginia, 72

Wage Record Interchange System, 38
Washington, D.C., 84
Washington Learns, 67
Washington State, 60, 61, 65, 72, 75, 77; Board for Community and Technical Colleges, 4, 59–60, 64, 74, 76, 77, 79; Office for Adult Basic Education, 65; Opportunity Grants, 66; two-year college system, 61; workforce, 63; Workforce Education Division, 65; Workforce Training and Education Coordinating Board, 66
Whittaker, D., 67
Wilson, B., 63
Windham, P., 3, 8, 37, 74
Winnick, S. Y., 77
Wisconsin, 50
Wisniewski, M., 53
Workforce Education and Training Board (Washington State), 65
Workforce Estimating Conference (Florida), 40
Workforce Investment Act, 85, 88

Zeidenberg, M., 74

Complete online access for your institution

Register for complimentary online access to *Journal of Leadership Studies* today!

Why Wait to Make Great Discoveries

Photography: Paweł Rosołek

4760

YOUR free ISSUE OF
NATIONAL CIVIC REVIEW
is now available online. Go to
www.interscience.wiley.com/journal/NCR

WILEY
InterScience®
DISCOVER SOMETHING GREAT

National Civic Review

- Get Sample Copy
- Recommend to Your Librarian
- Save journal to My Profile
- Set E-Mail Alert
- ✉ Email this page
- 🖨 Print this page

Special Issue
on Performance
Measurement
and Reporting

In this Issue:

- Public Employees as Partners in Performance: Lessons From the Field *by Brooke A. Myhre*
- Starting Performance Measurement From Outside Government in Worcester *by Roberta Schaefer*
- Current Approaches to Citizen Involvement in Performance Measurement and Questions They Raise *by Anne Spray Kinney*
- Bridging the Divide Between Community Indicators and Government Performance Measurement *by Ted Greenwood*

WILEY
Publishers Since 1807

OTHER TITLES AVAILABLE IN THE
NEW DIRECTIONS FOR COMMUNITY COLLEGES SERIES
Arthur M. Cohen, Editor-in-Chief
Richard L. Wagoner, Associate Editor

CC142 **Gendered Perspectives on Community College**
Jamie Lester
Gender-related conundrums lurk in every aspect of our society and culture,
and higher education is no exception. This volume explores and begins to
unravel the complexities of gender issues confronting men and women in
two-year institutions. The authors address a wide range of questions that
frame the current challenges facing community colleges, and they provide
thoughtful discussions of the gender-related experiences of female and male
students, staff, faculty, and administrators. The chapters blend evidence
from personal narratives and survey results and offer recommendations that
will help community colleges across the board, from serving students
struggling with identity issues to institutionalizing fairness in hiring and
promotion. The reader will come away with a better sense of how to assist
those who teach, learn, and lead in our nation's democratic colleges.
ISBN: 978-04073-72838

CC141 **Governance in the Community College**
Robert C. Cloud, Susan T. Kater
Community college governance is a process for distributing authority,
influence, and resources among internal and external constituencies. Having
evolved from traditional public school bureaucratic and political models that
emphasize control and oversight, community college governance is now a
dynamic process with a host of participants. Traditional governance models
will not suffice in this demanding arena. Governance structures that are
more collegial, flexible, and inclusive will be essential in the future as
community colleges evolve to meet the needs of an increasingly complex and
diverse society.
ISBN: 978-04703-21348

CC140 **The Current Landscape and Changing Perspectives of Part-Time Faculty**
Richard L. Wagoner
Community colleges are the only sector of public, nonprofit postsecondary
education in the United States where part-time faculty outnumber full-time
faculty. This has significant implications for community college administrators who are responsible for recruiting, hiring, and supporting part-time
faculty; for college, district, and state leaders who help set policies regarding
the use of part-timers; and for all part-time faculty who seek to receive
equitable treatment as they strive to enhance the quality of education for
community college students. This volume of *New Directions for Community
Colleges* seeks to encourage discussion and debate on the topic, to update
and advance the scholarship on part-time faculty, and to highlight best
practices and useful examples that can help two-year colleges continue
to play a vital role in American higher education.
ISBN: 978-04702-83578

NEW DIRECTIONS FOR COMMUNITY COLLEGES
Order Form
SUBSCRIPTIONS AND SINGLE ISSUES

DISCOUNTED BACK ISSUES:

Use this form to receive **20% off** all back issues of New Directions for Community Colleges. All single issues are priced at **$23.20** (normally $29.00).

TITLE	ISSUE NO.	ISBN
_____	_____	_____
_____	_____	_____
_____	_____	_____

Call 888-378-2537 or see mailing instructions below. When calling, mention the promotional code JB7ND to receive your discount.

SUBSCRIPTIONS: (1 year, 4 issues)

☐ New Order   ☐ Renewal

U.S.	☐ Individual: $80	☐ Institutional: $195
Canada/Mexico	☐ Individual: $80	☐ Institutional: $235
All Others	☐ Individual: $104	☐ Institutional: $269

Call 888-378-2537 or see mailing and pricing instructions below. Online subscriptions are available at www.interscience.wiley.com.

Copy or detach page and send to:
John Wiley & Sons, Journals Dept, 5th Floor
989 Market Street, San Francisco, CA 94103-1741

Order Form can also be faxed to: 888-481-2665

Issue/Subscription Amount: $ _____	**SHIPPING CHARGES:**		
Shipping Amount: $ _____	SURFACE	Domestic	Canadian
(for single issues only—subscription prices include shipping)	First Item	$5.00	$6.00
Total Amount: $ _____	Each Add'l Item	$3.00	$1.50

(No sales tax for U.S. subscriptions. Canadian residents, add GST for subscription orders. Individual rate subscriptions must be paid by personal check or credit card. Individual rate subscriptions may not be resold as library copies.)

☐ Payment enclosed (U.S. check or money order only. All payments must be in U.S. dollars.)

☐ VISA ☐ MC ☐ Amex # _____ Exp. Date _____

Card Holder Name _____ Card Issue # _____

Signature_____ Day Phone _____

☐ Bill Me (U.S. institutional orders only. Purchase order required.)

Purchase order # _____
Federal Tax ID13559302   GST 89102 8052

Name_____

Address _____

Phone _____ E-mail _____

JB7ND